MILLIONAIRE MUMPRENEURS

How Successful Mums Made a Million Online
and How You Can Do it Too!

by Mel McGee

HARRIMAN HOUSE LTD

3A Penns Road
Petersfield
Hampshire
GU32 2EW
GREAT BRITAIN

Tel: +44 (0)1730 233870
Fax: +44 (0)1730 233880
Email: enquiries@harriman-house.com
Website: www.harriman-house.com

First published in Great Britain in 2010
Copyright © Harriman House Ltd

The right of Mel McGee to be identified as Author has been asserted in accordance
with the Copyright, Design and Patents Act 1988.

ISBN: 978-1906659-61-5

British Library Cataloguing in Publication Data
A CIP catalogue record for this book can be obtained from the British Library.

Photos: Alexis - copyright www.bohmphotography.com
Elizabeth - copyright www.bohmphotography.com
Fabienne - copyright www.clientattraction.com
Janet - copyright Janet Beckers www.janetbeckers.com
Karen - copyright Karen Knowler www.therawfoodcoach.com
Sheri - copyright Sheri McConnell www.sherimcconnell.com

Printed and bound by the CPI Group Antony Rowe, Chippenham

Dedicated to you

Supporting Mums and Children

10% of author royalties are donated to charities
supporting mothers and children.

CONTENTS

ACKNOWLEDGEMENTS

A huge thank you to all the inspirational women who have been so supportive, honest and generous in sharing their story and without whom this book couldn't have been written:

Karen Knowler, Janet Beckers, Elizabeth Potts Weinstein, Alexis Martin Neely, Fabienne Fredrickson and Sheri McConnell.

Your collective wisdom has shown me that it's possible to be a mum, have passion for what you do, enjoy building a hugely successful online business from home and be a wonderful person. I'm honoured.

To Myles Hunt, Suzanne Anderson and Louise Hinchen at Harriman House publishing and Helen McCusker at Booked PR – an amazing team. Thanks for believing in me and helping me get my message out there. Your support, cooperation and guidance have made it a pleasure working with you.

To Debbie Jenkins and Joe Gregory at Lean Marketing Press for giving me one of my first breaks. Cheers!

To all the supportive mumpreneurs and business women and men I have connected with online and in the real world and to all my loyal Supermummy subscribers, clients and members. Thinking of you.

To my community of friends, family and husband Terry. Thanks for putting up with me!

And last but not least, to my kids Aimee, Emilee and Mickey. You are the sunshine of my life. XXX

MEL MCGEE

SUPERMUMMY

ABOUT THE AUTHOR

Mel McGee is the founder of Supermummy and is the UK's voice for mumpreneurs. Her website at www.supermummy.com offers online business success solutions for mums, a mumpreneur social network and a radio show. She's an NLP (neuro-linguistic programming) Master Practitioner and runs her virtual business from her home office in Herefordshire where she lives with her husband and three children. Mel's passion is to help change the way mums work and to make running an online business from home a realistic option for today's women.

FOREWORD

I know how you feel because I've been there too. I'm a successful business woman now but it wasn't always this way. I first started out on my entrepreneurial journey as a young single mother with no job or prospects and still living at home with my mum. My drive and ambition came from a need to provide for my son, to inspire and encourage him. By taking action and having the determination to follow through on an idea, I appeared on Channel 4's *Make Me A Million* with my 'Halos n Horns' chemical-free children's toiletries, and won. So whatever situation you're in now, you too can make your business dream a reality.

What I love about Mel's book is the 'can-do' attitude and the emphasis on solutions to combining work and family. She has really raised awareness to the unprecedented opportunity that technology and the internet provides for building a business from home. Mums have always been resourceful with ways to make money after having children but this book is about serious business that gives you family time too.

We can't 'play' at business and expect to be taken seriously and Mel explains the importance of setting clear boundaries for work time and family time. Being an entrepreneurial mum of three and implementing many of the strategies in her Supermummy business, Mel knows what she is talking about. She has a compelling style that makes the information easy to understand. Her book's a great combination of online business strategies, coaching and success stories, providing you with lots of inspiration.

I'm on my third business venture and I've learned how important it is to delegate. You simply can't go on doing everything yourself, so this along with letting go of any guilt will help you make progress. Mel has shown that running a business from home isn't necessarily a case of extreme multitasking, it's more about getting the right support around you.

Women gain strength from hearing success stories and reading this book felt like actually meeting Mel and the other mumpreneurs in person. Whether you are just thinking about starting up in business or are already up and running, this book is ideal as a guide you can refer to again and again for strategies and inspiration. If enough mums read this book and wholeheartedly implement what they have learned, it could give a whole new meaning to flexible working from home – for yourself!

Leila Wilcox

January 2010

PREFACE

My name is Mel McGee. I am the founder of Supermummy, a company dedicated to empowering mums to build a successful online business from home that fits with their family life. My website at www.supermummy.com offers information, education, support and products. As a mum of three young children I needed a business that would give me freedom and flexibility, so I set out to find a way to build an online business for purpose, pleasure and profit. With no experience in business, no technical expertise, little money and even less time I slowly but surely made the transition from stressed-out mum working full-time, to frustrated stay-at-home mum, to entrepreneurial mum working from home. I've made mistakes along the way and felt like throwing in the towel many times, but like all rollercoasters the dips don't last long and the highs are always worth it. On my journey I was delighted to discover that there were mums who were not only proving that running an online business from home could be done already, but some of them were making millions. I was hooked and the more I learned about them the more I realised that all of you needed to know about them too.

The more I found out about these inspirational mumpreneurs who were building purposeful, authentic and successful online businesses, the more I knew that I had to write a book about them. *Millionaire Mumpreneurs* is different. It's a combination of business, self-help and success. I wrote it to introduce you to these savvy women, to share their stories and mine too, to show you how their online businesses differ from others and to demonstrate that what's possible for them is possible for you. You just need to know how!

Here's to our success!

Mel x

"Here's to the crazy ones, the misfits, the rebels, the troublemakers, the round pegs in the square holes, the ones who see things differently – they're not fond of rules. You can quote them, disagree with them, glorify or vilify them, but the only thing you can't do is ignore them because they change things... they push the human race forward and, while some may see them as the crazy ones, we see genius, because the ones who are crazy enough to think that they can change the world, are the ones who do."

'Think Different', Apple Inc marketing campaign, 1997

INTRODUCTION

There's no going back! Now, more than ever, our lives are being shaped by technology and the growth rate of the internet exceeds that of any previous technology. Today the internet is expanding exponentially in size, processing power and software sophistication. People are increasingly accessing the internet from mobile phones, broadband penetration in the UK is soaring, and thanks to higher speed connections it just gets quicker and easier to go online.

The internet has changed the way we communicate. By the end of 2009, social networking site Facebook's user base had grown to over 300 million, which is nearly as large as the US population (307 million). Like Facebook, Twitter has experienced phenomenal growth and new networking and social media sites keep launching. According to Neilsen Online, the growth of internet users in Europe between 2000 and 2009 was 282%, with 52% of the European population being users, compared to 74.2% in North America. Cisco Systems predicts that over the next few years the internet will grow by 500%. Google now a corporate superpower, gets billions of searches each month worldwide and supercharges how we get our information.

In addition to searching for information and communicating online we also spend money online, we fall in love online through dating sites, we express our opinions online through blogs and we broadcast ourselves online through sites like YouTube. Yes, the downside is that it's absolutely possible to become a 'web addict', but, used in the right way, the internet is most certainly an empowering tool. Let's celebrate that and see how the internet offers an unprecedented opportunity for business success for mums wanting to work without sacrificing too much family time.

My journey of building a virtual business from home has been both fascinating and frustrating. Frustrating because of the exhaustive amount of information to evaluate. Fascinating because after filtering all the hype and choosing your contacts, friends and mentors you can benefit hugely from new voices, new conversations, new faces and new ways of thinking that will help you expand your world. All from the comfort of your own home!

Getting close to successful people and understanding how and why they do what they do has always been a key success strategy. Thanks to the internet, now, more than ever, it's possible to learn from and connect with extraordinary people who can influence and inspire you. Without the internet and technology it would have been incredibly hard for me to reach all the women in this book and discover their stories. Since the interviews I have had the opportunity to meet them all in 'real life' and I'm happy to report that they are just like you and me. Some of them are now turning over multi-millions, yet their businesses look different to most; there's no boardroom, no layers of management, no commuting, and no power suit. The difference lies in the way they think and their business approach. The internet has made it possible for them to market themselves, deliver their services and scale their businesses in a way that simply wasn't possible before.

Many life-changing events can be triggered by a single decision, perhaps involving a relationship, that dreamed-of job, or starting a family. It's never been easy for mums to make the 'right' decision about whether to work or how to be there for the kids and contribute to the family finances too. A Tesco survey showed that half of working mums have considered setting up their own business because it gives them much more flexibility than a corporate job. A Working Mums (www.workingmums.co.uk) survey revealed that women are now less likely than ever to maintain a full-time job after having children, with 24% working full-time and 60% working part-time. A factor was that 83% of mums found it hard to find flexible jobs which used their skills, and 55% would prefer to work from home.

So what about those that take the plunge? Many talented women from UK plc are shunning corporate life to start family-friendly businesses. But how many more are sat at their desks spending every working day trying to figure out a way to work from home and make a good living thinking, 'There's got to be more to life than this'? Are you one of them? Maybe you are struck by 'analysis paralysis' and are waiting for something to happen? More time? More money? More energy? Maybe you have convinced yourself that starting a business from home would be too hard or you anticipate too many problems. So you just stay put and wait. But for what?

Some mums just know that they're ready to take the leap of faith and go it alone. They're at the gates saying, "Let me out! I'm ready!" There are certainly more and more of them deciding to set up as a home business. The *2009 Home Business Report* from Enterprise Nation uncovered the growth in the number of home-based businesses, with over 1,400 starting up each week and the highest growth coming from mums, young people and the over 50s. So a home-based business, the report says, is a route to bringing people into employment who otherwise might not have contributed to the economy.

I wrote this book as my way of contributing and getting the message out there. It's how I can inspire mums who want to know how to go about building a virtual business from home and how they too can create their ideal flexible lifestyle. You'll get a very different perspective on working from home from this book. This isn't about get-rich-quick schemes on the internet. It's not about selling stuff on eBay. It's not about having an online shop full of dropshipped items. It's about building a successful and flexible business run from home, that uses your skills and creativity and that fits around your busy family life. The material in this book is a combination of my own experiences and those of other mums around the world who have proven the dream is possible. These amazing women have all created meaningful, purposeful businesses from scratch. Each of them has shared their success story with you and me. One of them might have started out in a similar position or with a similar background to yours. They didn't have all the answers when they started out, they didn't have enough time, and they didn't know how it was going to work out, but they have made a success of their business while keeping their priorities (their families) intact. Advances in technology have given them a way to follow their passion, do meaningful work they love and have the freedom and flexibility for family life, and that's why I want to share their success strategies with you. Consider this book a launch guide to help you plan your new venture.

HOW ARE YOU FEELING?

If you're feeling stuck right now, I know how you feel. I felt stuck when I was working full-time after having my first baby but I also felt stuck when I was a stay-at-home mum after my second baby. I guess the grass is always greener, but maybe it doesn't have to be so cut and dry. Maybe removing the fence is the ideal place to start. We can stay at home, work at what we love doing and be financially independent. We can do both right now. Are you ready to change the paradigm and the way you work and live?

Have you got what it takes to be a millionaire mumpreneur? Is entrepreneurship really the right path for you? Imagine taking responsibility for your working life and never again having to fit into a role at work, get sidetracked in your career or accept a job you are overqualified and underpaid for because the hours fit with the school run. Consider the freedom to express the real you and not having to apologise for having kids because now, as an entrepreneur, you can create a business around your family priorities. Within this book you have the combined knowledge and success secrets from experts that have done this – but what are you going to do with this information? Are you going to act now and change the way you work and live or are you going to put it on the shelf while you think about it? Building a business like the mums in this book could give you freedom and potentially make you a millionaire, but only if you can take the first step. Is there a millionaire mumpreneur (MM) inside you?

HAVING IT ALL AND BEING IT ALL BY NOT DOING IT ALL!

Yes, it can be done. You can be there for your partner and family, have some 'me' time and have your dream job. You just have to create it yourself! You can have it all, you can be it all but you certainly don't have to do it all, and the MMs that you will read about in this book have proven that it's possible to build a business that fits with family life, meaning you can keep your priorities intact *and* still contribute financially. They have families to care for and homes to run just like you, but now they have successful businesses on top, So just how do they do it? By building a team. You'll learn more about this key factor later but I want to get the point across now that this isn't about taking on more and more responsibility until you are a nervous breakdown waiting to happen. This is about letting go of guilt, martyrdom and multitasking, and embracing delegation. It's less about working for yourself and more about having others do the work for you, leaving you with the work you really love to do. Yes, you'll probably need some childcare, but working this way means you don't have to be out of the home 60 hours a week and too knackered to play at the weekends. You could be delighted to discover that you can actually get a lot done working 20 hours a week on your business from home. If like some of the MMs in this book you would prefer your children to be cared for or schooled at home while you get some work done then that's an option too. What's possible for them is possible for you. You just need to know how.

Perhaps the gap seems too wide from where you are now, to being in a position of running a successful business; and you can't see how you can get to that place yet. First you need to know where you want to be in order to plan how to get there, and being a mum working from home need not be perceived as a weakness in a business plan. In fact, you can leverage being an online business by investing in the latest technology, automated systems and outsourcing any support you need, thereby eliminating the cost of employees and business premises. The *2009 Home Business Report* from Enterprise Nation also says:

> Technology remains a key enabler to starting and growing a business from home and home businesses are early adopters of social media, with 81% of survey respondents stating that technology is critical to the success of their business and 74% using social networking sites to keep in touch with other businesses.

By stripping away inflexible strategies such as leasing premises and hiring full-time employees you can create a company that is always poised for change and creativity.

Do you feel like you are reaching your potential now? In your job? In your personal life? As a parent? Probably not! People are searching for meaning and purpose in their lives more than ever and this is becoming increasingly evident in the business world. Before, it was mega brands and big faceless companies but now it's small companies with big hearts, minds and vision. These MMs have pursued their dream with purpose, dared to work differently and are helping to set a new standard for flexible working for mums all over the world. For us.

STOP MULTITASKING

Perhaps you feel torn that by being a working mum you are not giving your best at work or at home and think that being your own boss will be an easy way out. Becoming an entrepreneur can certainly give you the freedom and flexibility you need but to get the security of an income you must take it seriously and not try to multitask like crazy when you are working from home.

But what about my children?

I have already mentioned the need for childcare and this is going to be a fundamental part of your plan. How are you going to work on a business whilst caring for your children? With great difficulty, take it from me! You might just get away with checking a few emails or posting a quick update on social media while your children are temporarily occupied, but the real, productive work will require 100% of your focus. What about working in the evenings? Your children go to sleep much earlier than you giving you a few hours of uninterrupted time, right? Well yes, in theory, working on your business in the evenings may seem like your best option to start with. But I would suggest that it's not a situation that is realistic and sustainable, especially if you're frazzled after a long day. Get to a point as quickly as you can whereby your business is what you do during the day and evenings are for relaxing (or perhaps even a bit of socialising!).

To be a success you must set up crystal clear boundaries right from the start to prevent yourself from being completely overwhelmed and exhausted. If running a business from home gives you the option to cut down on childcare and be more available for your kids then you'll have to just knuckle down while your kids are in childcare, school or with someone you trust. You need to be more self-disciplined than ever, which also means no procrastinating or being distracted by the laundry, TV, phone or fridge. The hours in which your children are in childcare, at school, etc, is your time to work on your business and *nothing else.*

Remember: you are un-multitasking here and want to get yourself into a position of delegating as quickly as possible. The simple tasks like answering calls, administration and bookkeeping can easily be outsourced if they are distracting you from the productive work. It sounds scary, but you can do this! There are lots of people, many of them mums themselves, offering their services, so look into it.

It's your decision

Ultimately any change starts with a decision and once you have made the decision to get started then you'll need to follow through on that decision, which will require consistent action. Your success will not be down to luck. It will be a result of your consistent efforts to grow your business and how quickly that happens will come down to how you think and what you do. These MMs all started by taking a decision. They weren't dabbling, or doing a bit of moonlighting or thinking, "I'll do this until I get a proper job when the kids are older".

Now, I'm not suggesting you go and hand your notice in tomorrow, you are currently a mum employed. Starting out in this kind of business doesn't mean you have to give up your current source of income, but if you are going to do it on the side then you must be committed. The MMs took their commitment seriously, persevered and in doing so sent out a powerful message. Playing at a business will not get you massive results. Setting out with a purpose and doing something you love is important, but if you don't start to take your business seriously, sooner or later you will not only be preventing it from growing but you'll be running yourself ragged trying to do it all. You must set out to master it, succeed and stay focused on the vision you have for yourself and your life.

> **" The hours in which your children are in childcare, at school, etc. is your time to work on your business. "**

THINK DIFFERENTLY

These MMs are stepping up bigger and bolder than before. They have learned, sometimes the hard way, the fundamentals of running a business and have put the infrastructure in place to support the growth of their virtual companies; and that's the secret. Because their businesses are primarily information-based they have been able to exploit technology to deliver many of their services in a virtual way. Adopting a more virtual approach means you don't necessarily need to meet with your clients face-to-face to deliver your service, so now you can reach tens, hundreds, even thousands more people. In essence they have moved away from being paid for the amount of hours they work to being paid many times over for the same service.

How it works

Let me explain further how this differs from the 'traditional' service business. As you know, in any consulting or service business people pay you for your services. So if you wanted to, say, double your income, you would have to either have to double your fees or double the amount of clients. If you increase your fees you'll eventually reach a maximum level where new clients will drop off or you will be overpriced compared to your competitors, so your only option then is to work more hours serving more clients or to hire employees to serve some of those clients. However, what if you could provide that information/consultancy by delivering that information through your website? You could be providing, say, an audio-based service to 100 clients at a time on a conference call, or via a video service with a webinar. You could package some of the most valuable information into eBooks or design an online or home-study course.

I'll expand more on these strategies later, but at this stage I want you to start imagining what your business could look like. By 'multiplying yourself' and leveraging what you know, you can easily duplicate your results over and over again without duplicating your hours worked. Now I know that this might sound too good to be true or be hard for you to accept; you may even be thinking that this is simply laziness because our society seems to applaud hard work over personal productivity. But, working this way means cutting out a lot of non-productive time at work, like commuting, hanging around the office cooler, meetings to discuss meetings, etc. Choosing to do work from home that you find meaningful and important can be far more fulfilling *and* productive.

Are you satisfied?

Although these virtual teaching methods are nothing new, the concept of implementing these strategies in a home business may not be something you had considered feasible. First, you must believe that it's possible for you to work this way before you start making plans. After all, if you don't believe any of this applies to your business or business idea then the chances are you will be reluctant to even test a few ideas. The MMs sharing their success stories in this book are like you in so many ways but they probably think very differently, and that is the key. Feeling completely satisfied and fulfilled with the way you live and work sounds fantastic but what makes us feel that way? Being a millionaire? No, this is less about making money and more about having the freedom and choice about what we do with our lives. That's the real power. Critical to any entrepreneur's success is thinking differently.

These MMs have found fulfilment inside the home, are making a difference and they know what they are working for. It's not just for the money! They may not have made a difference to your world but to the many people they serve through their businesses, to the people they pay to support them, to the people they collaborate with and to their children's lives, they've made great contributions. They could make a difference to your life by being a role model for combining a successful business with family life. They have remained true to themselves and you'll be delighted to discover that they started out close to where you might be right now. Yes, they all had to learn from some painful experiences but they all took the time and made the effort to inform and educate themselves. They didn't leave their success to fate, to chance, to hope. They didn't sit and worry about 'what if?' for too long. Learning the way from these real-life inspirational stories before you set out on your mumpreneur journey could help you avoid the pitfalls and understand how your business could work for you.

IT'S JUST A QUESTION OF 'HOW'

Success comes down to how-to strategies, not luck, and modelling success strategies can give you a shortcut to results. Modelling is simply understanding what someone is doing and their strategies, and following the same pattern. Modelling can be a combination of actions, behaviours and thinking processes; think of it as a recipe. Let's say you want to bake an apple pie just like Grandma's. There are the obvious elements like the basic ingredients, but she might have a specific order in which she adds them, a certain style of kneading the dough, a special ingredient – she may even have to be in the right emotional state! What's important is that she gets the same or very similar results every time she bakes that apple pie.

The recipe for success

You need to discover what successful people do well (or not, as the case may be) to help you have similar success in your business. Modelling is not the same as copying; you are not going to go out and completely clone someone's business to get the same results. That's a strategy for failure (and potentially a legal battle)! Look at your potential model's results, at what they have achieved and who they are, and if you find yourself thinking, 'That's just what I want' then you've found a great role model and you can get to work discovering how they achieved their end results. You can then master the strategies that they use for success and apply them in your unique business, compressing what may have taken them decades to achieve into just a few years, or even months.

Understanding and applying the success strategies you'll learn about in this book could be the quickest way for you to get from where you are now to where you really want to be. It could save you time, money and energy, and stop you making the same mistakes. From these MM stories I've extracted the success strategies that have specifically contributed to their phenomenal results. You won't be learning about standard business practicalities required by all businesses such as tax advice, accounting, invoicing, and payroll, etc, although they are, of course, important and I recommend you consult with your local business advice service. My point is that you won't find what *I'm* writing about in general business start-up advice resources. I want to show you how resourceful you can be when you know how. I believe that women especially gain strength by learning from other, experienced women and that inspires us to make changes in our lives.

But I'm so busy

What? Too busy? "Mel, I'd love to read these stories of how these Superwomen have built these amazing businesses and are living their dream lives but some of us are just too exhausted and drowning in nappies and chores and have to do a 'proper job' whether we like it or not and put up with the drudgery and just get on with it and I'm just too busy to make it happen anyway." Remember: busy is not the same as productive. We can spend all day every day being 'busy' and being a businesses owner will quickly help you to see the difference. It's going to take some self-examination and decision-making but perhaps it won't be as tough to pull it off as you are imagining it will be. What I know for sure is that the technology is there to help us build businesses from home and have a huge client base, and there has never been a better time for us to exploit that. We're all in this together!

"RAW SUCCESS"

Karen Knowler is the Raw Food Coach (www.therawfoodcoach.com) and former managing director of the Fresh Network (www.fresh-network.com), a top UK raw and living foods organisation. Karen's story is a great example of how you can transition your skills from a previous career to a business of your own. With 16 years' personal experience of eating a raw-food diet, Karen has been teaching, writing and coaching professionally about raw foods for over a decade. Co-author of *Feel-good Food* and author of *Raw Food for Begineers*. Karen's extensive knowledge and experience of all issues relating to raw food eating, as well as her accessible, positive and inspiring take on 'eating for energy' also make her a role model for making a living from a passion. That passion for raw foods is based on her personal transformation from, "pudgy junk-food addict and butcher's shop worker to slim-line superwoman and raw-food visionary". Single mum Karen is based in Cambridgeshire in the UK but now has clients all over the world who have attended her classes and training courses, followed her recipes, bought her resources and participated in her coaching programmes. She manages to run her successful business from home with the support of two assistants. Karen is well on the way to making her first million from the Raw Food Coach, but how did it all start?

KAREN'S STORY

For many years Karen was managing director of the Fresh Network so was already working in an industry she was passionate about. Let's find out more about when and why she left:

"It all started back in 1998 when I took on the ownership of a company called the Fresh Network, the first organisation promoting raw food in the UK. I'd been a member of it since 1993 and was always gently pestering the owner for a job, but it didn't make any money at the time and it came to a point when she wanted to let go of the business and let someone else take over. The Fresh Network was making low profits and was a very home-spun business but I was so passionate about raw food and something just told me to be the one to take it on. It was really hard work. I started off running it in my spare time and then life conspired to put me in a situation that made me jump off the cliff! I had a job in PR but found very quickly that it was not for me, so I basically took a leap of faith and said, "I'm going to put everything into building the Fresh Network up. I've got one month's salary to live on and if I don't start making money within those first four weeks and get signs that this is viable then I'll just go and temp again". Fortunately I had limited responsibilities at the time. I was still scared as hell but I took that leap of faith because I thought if I don't do it now I never will. I worked my tush off for the Fresh Network and turned it around into a really successful business."

You could easily think that Karen had a great head start for the Raw Food Coach from her experience at the Fresh Network, but what's interesting is Karen's honesty about her lack of confidence going it alone under her own name. Karen explains:

Get over it

"The Fresh Network gave me a platform in the raw-food community, so people knew who I was but I was always hiding behind the company name. When I sold the company in February 2007, the Raw Food Coach site had only been live since September 2006, and going for it under my own name really affected my confidence. I felt a lot of fear, even though I'd been working in the raw-food field for years. I thought, 'What if people are only interested in the Fresh Network and not me?' I now know, through coaching other business owners, that everyone goes through a lack of confidence. You very rarely meet a person that doesn't have major hang ups! So it's perfectly normal and natural, but the bottom line is that you have to get over it. I think that's one of the key secrets to my success with the Raw Food Coach, because it has been much more successful than the Fresh Network. It's absolutely all about marketing, knowing how that works and how to promote in a way that feels good and is done with integrity and not hype.

"On an inner level, it's about being committed to serving people and being so passionate about the message that you have to get yourself out of the way. I see so many people sitting at their desks worrying about marketing, but it's not about you. It's about the people you're trying to serve and if you use all your energy being wrapped up in your fear or ego or your sense of self, that's the biggest disservice you can give to the people you serve because your energy is in the wrong place. I didn't know how right that was until I started coaching people who were really struggling, because for me I just had to get the message out. I'm coaching people now who say "Yes, but I don't *want* to be seen". Well, if you don't want to be seen then you're in the wrong business because you've got to be seen. Don't confuse yourself with the message because people are only interested in the message. As much as we would love to think that people are fascinated with us as an individual, they're not. They're interested in what we can do for them. Hopefully that helps people get over that hurdle."

From this experience Karen is passionate about helping others see how getting in their own way is sabotaging their success. She describes how thinking of herself as a 'vehicle for information' takes away any self-consciousness:

A vehicle for information

" I understand people sometimes have their own neuroses, but I see their message and I see the way they can benefit people. I think that one of the reasons the Raw Food Coach has been so successful is because I really committed to just being a vehicle for information. My best programme ideas and my best offerings come from this place all the time. It's just how it is for me now.

T. Harv Eker said:

> *If you're not earning enough, it's because you're not serving enough people.*

" And that has made the biggest impact on me out of anything I've ever heard about business, because any time my funds have run low, or they're about to, I have asked myself, "Am I serving enough people?" And, of course, the answer is going to be no, so I get the message out in a bigger way. In the early days we all start off with a handful of customers, but when we really grow and become more confident then we need to grow beyond serving just a few people.

" I've seen that for myself and now every time I go into any kind of comfort zone, I suffer. I've launched a 12-month programme and it's the biggest thing I've ever done. Usually my programmes are only open to 30 or 40 people, but this one shouldn't be capped because this is amazing, life-changing stuff, so the more people the better! Consequently, out of all the coaching programmes that I've ever run in my entire business history, this has already grossed more money than anything else I've done before. "

Let's go back to what Karen was doing when she was first online. We need to understand the first steps she took and how she expanded into the coaching of today. It all started with a blog:

In the beginning

"I actually started off with my blog, in October 2005. I was blogging to express myself because I could feel myself shifting and outgrowing the Fresh Network. There were things I wanted to talk about and the Fresh Network wasn't giving me the vehicle to do that, so I started blogging quite prolifically because I love writing. My blog attracted an increasing number of readers and I then added a sign-up box so people could get their names down before my first ezine [email newsletter] was published. My ezine came out just before I launched my website, which was great because I actually had something to sell. I remember the first time I sold an eBook; I was jumping up and down with glee. That first eBook has gone on to sell thousands. It gave me the feedback I needed that people did actually want to buy my information.

"Historically, I have been overly generous by giving stuff away all the time, which was nearly the death of the company because I would hold back on price increases and it just didn't make sound business sense. What really appeals to me about internet marketing is that you can still give a lot away but it's via your website rather than a physical product or your time. You can actually be very benevolent and generous. Another mistake people make is to withhold their best tips and advice for the paying customers, but unless we put great information out there, people can't see what we can provide. That's a classic error; people hold back with their material but then don't get the clients because people aren't seeing what they have to give."

Of course your website has to have traffic in order for people to sign up for your ezine or buy your eBook and it seems that all the blogging Karen was doing about raw food was helping to push her site to the top of Google. Unbeknown to her at the time, people searching 'raw foods' were easily finding the Raw Food Coach:

" Blogging really helped me in the Google rankings. I think I even went to number one for 'raw foods' because I'd been writing about it so much. At the time, I didn't even know that could happen, but suddenly raw foods and Karen Knowler were synonymous. When my first website went live I was sending my ezine to almost 200 people. Today my subscriber list is at 13,500 and growing. "

Let's find out more about how Karen is actually making money from her business. After all, a free email newsletter and one eBook probably won't pay the bills. So how did she expand?

Revenue streams

" I have several eBooks and a home-study programme for raw-food professionals. I also offer business coaching and train others in the raw-foods community. I'm coming away from one-to-one coaching but I now work with group programmes. The raw-foods niche is really growing and training others is an additional revenue stream. I was the best person, as far as I know, to put themselves out there as the most experienced raw-food coach. If you have that credibility then you shouldn't hide it because it's damaging to your business as it doesn't let other people know how much you have to offer. I still ask myself: "Who are you to say this?" But if I was coaching someone else with the same amount of experience and expertise, I would say they were mad not to tell the world because they have so much to give. You have to analyse it from the outside, then go forth and tell people! Although my niche is raw foods I have unintentionally become one of the best business coaches in the UK. I've invested in my education and have put it all back into my work and my business. "

At what point was it that Karen made the decision to invest in herself, giving her the knowledge and confidence to really grow her business?

Karen explains how things improved when she changed her perception of marketing.

Marketing is being a nuisance

" I saw people marketing really well in the field of raw foods but I wasn't because I felt that marketing was being a pain or a nuisance to people. I was very self-conscious around the whole thing until I heard Jay Abraham say:

> *If you're not telling people what you do you're doing them a disservice.*

That really affected me because I wanted to be of service, so to hear that my lack of marketing was actually doing a disservice was the wake-up call I needed. As soon as I understood what marketing was about and how it could be of benefit, it became the most logical and the most intelligent thing for me to invest my time and money in. "

What strategies have proven the most effective for Karen while building her virtual business?

Giving from the heart

" I was always so clear about my ezine. It is there to give really high-quality content. My ezine is my direct contact with my audience; it's there to connect with them, it's there to tell them what's going on with me, and it's there to give them something of great value like an article and a recipe. The content really should be paid for but there's no expectation of that from me. I am here to serve and my generosity has come back to me.

" Doing an ezine is one great strategy, but YouTube has also been phenomenal for me. I've had over 400,000 visits of my YouTube videos (www.youtube.com/karenknowler) over the past two years; it's been incredible and the irony is that I only put up some clips because people wanted to see recipes being taught and there's only so many people I can have in a live class. YouTube is a great medium for being filmed in my own kitchen making recipes, and as a result people would get to know me better. As mentioned earlier, blogging was another great strategy.

"At the end of the day, as consumers we are all the same. We want to see and connect with the people that seem to care, even if they don't personally know us. They're giving valuable information seemingly without an agenda. Yes we want to make money but we don't have to worry about that if we're leading with generosity first. Just know that the more you give the more you get."

So, after starting out selling a simple eBook, Karen has progressed into raw-food training courses and classes, information products and membership to her coaching programmes. Responding to the needs of her clients she has also expanded into business coaching for other raw food professionals. After all that work, what kind of results has Karen seen from the Raw Food Coach so far? In other words, how much has she made?

Changing my relationship with money

"In, 2007, my first year, I made bang on £100,000, which was incredible. In 2009 I made about £400,000 from the Raw Food Coach. I want to inspire people because I used to have lots of money hang-ups and I've had to grow and change my relationship with money in order to be comfortable around it. I'm happy talking about it now but I used to have very limiting and negative beliefs. Much of my personal work has focused on overcoming that. Now, the more money I make means the more people I can and have helped.

"For each person it's about finding what really drives them. It's not always about money in the bank because that doesn't do that much good. If you are drawn to service and you really want to make the world a better place, you have to realise that money is the tool that's going to help you do so. If you can't manage money, if you don't feel comfortable with money, and

> " **In 2009 I made about £400,000 from the Raw Food Coach.** "

if you don't charge what you're worth, then you will hinder your capacity to do what you came here to do. I've had to learn this and so will you. "

Not bad for starting with a free blog! Of course, planning, developing and launching new products and programmes takes a considerable amount of time and effort. How has Karen managed all that whilst also being a mum?

Hiring the right people

" I'm a single mum now, but during the early years my partner and I alternated the childcare so that got us through the first stage. Then my partner moved 300 miles away, which rendered me a single mum in every sense of the word. It was tough but I took on my assistant, Katie, and she's been amazing. She works full-time in my house in a separate office. Hiring ideal people is critical though not necessarily easy; I had to learn big lessons about not just hiring nice people but hiring the right people.

" My son's father moved back in with me in 2009. We're not a couple; it's an arrangement that's unusual but it has worked. For me, the point of growing a business is also to create a good lifestyle for myself and for my son. I'm putting key people in place so that I can be in a position to spend more time with my son. During the school holidays his dad is with him. I'm at my desk but I can go and see him whenever I want during the day, and I have more time and money to spend with him at the weekends. "

Karen has emphasised the importance of having the right team to support you. Since our interview she has now taken on another assistant and this is how her team looks.

The Raw Food team

"In addition to Katie, I work with three different designers, three different web people, someone who's doing some writing for me, plus I have a marketing VA (virtual assistant) who helps me strategise launches and writes copy for affiliate promotions. I have an online shopping cart VA, a travel consultant who sorts out the best deals for my flights as currently I'm travelling to the US on a regular basis, an accountant and bookkeeper all in one, and I used to have a housekeeper. My preference is to have a team in-house and I'm looking to achieve this. Sometimes it has to be virtual, but I have found that having Katie here in the building makes things far easier."

Home alone

This virtual world is fascinating and very different from many people's perception of what flexible working entails. Working part-time at a job that fits in with school hours is a complete contrast to being the director of your own company but still having the flexibility to do the school run. What does Karen talk about at the school gates? Does she ever feel isolated from other mums in her community? She doesn't currently have a peer group in her local community, and because she chooses to travel to the US on a regular basis for business it also seems that not many people truly understand what she is doing.

In my experience I have found working from home to be isolating at times, especially on the days when you really crave the kind of adult company you get in a working environment compared to a playgroup, but I know that I can easily solve that issue and create opportunities to get out more in 'the real world' if that's what I need. On the flip side there have been many more times when I have been so happy to be working from home, casually dressed at my desk with only a few hours of childcare required to allow me to get everything done. But if you've never worked from home before, even as an employee, do you need to be a certain type of person and how do you keep yourself motivated? Karen says:

Every coach has a coach

"I've always loved my own company and I actually love working from home. I'm quite happy being on my own all day. I have coached someone who was building a virtual business but she went back to the mainstream workplace because she missed not being around people. Until that happened with her I didn't realise that it was a possibility. You need to have a different mindset and I go to places like the US to mix with like-minded people. Most people don't understand what I do and that's why every coach has a coach. I have invested hugely in my personal mentoring and coaching. Before, I was spinning my wheels and going crazy because I knew I was ready for more and I needed a mentor to pull me through. I have really grown and I also learned first-hand what I am capable of. It's compelled me to step-up both personally and professionally, and I can serve in an even better way because I have much more confidence."

Karen's story proves that it's possible to make a great living by building a business around something you are passionate about. The health industry is full of magazines, websites, professionals and products, yet Karen succeeded in the small niche of raw foods. By taking an innovative approach she has established her position as one of the UK's top raw-food professionals and has attracted clients worldwide. Karen doesn't just talk the talk, she has eaten a mostly or all raw-food-diet since 1993, and has certainly opened my eyes to what you can do with nut milk! If you have a related passion or already work in a similar industry, consider how you could follow Karen's example.

> **" It's possible to make a great living by building a business around something you are passionate about. "**

"TURNING PASSION
INTO PROFITS"

JANET'S STORY

Janet Beckers seemed to come out of nowhere but she is leading the way for women wanting to learn about internet marketing or who wish to get access to inspirational role models. Janet is the founder of Wonderful Web Women (www.wonderfulwebwomen.com), an award-winning community of women (and enlightened men) around the world who help each other create online success.

On the day that Janet launched Wonderful Web Women she had no clients, no money and no track record. Within eight weeks she had built a worldwide community of thousands, matched her previous 12 months' income, and won an award for best membership site. She is now a sought-after international speaker and author. She has also just been awarded 'Australian Marketer of the Year' by the Marketing Communications Executives International organisation.

Janet has inspired thousands of people worldwide to follow their dreams and realise their potential by building a profitable online business based on their passions. Her thriving virtual business has a team spread throughout Australia and overseas, all managed by phone and email from Janet's home-based office in her sunroom. This gives her the flexibility to spend lots of time with her two children and ecologist husband at their home in a small beachside community on the New South Wales Central Coast, and even have the time to care for a new puppy!

Janet has succeeded in creating the ideal internet lifestyle business she wanted, but Wonderful Web Women wasn't actually Janet's first online venture. Her first experience in business was a different story. Janet explains how it all happened.

'Overnight' success

"I launched Wonderful Web Women in August 2007, and went from nobody knowing me, having no clients or prospects and no product, to very quickly becoming known worldwide because of the strategy that I used. I established myself as the 'go-to' person in my niche (internet marketing) by interviewing the most successful women in the world who had created their success online. As well as helping me create an information product (the recordings of the interview) they promoted me to their list of subscribers, and this is what built my list so quickly. All the wonderful people the interviewees referred to me had to subscribe to my list to get the details of the interview by tele-seminar. They could participate in the calls for free, but the call recordings and lots of other great resources were only available to paying members of Wonderful Web Women. The business has grown from there.

"People assumed that I had all of a sudden hit the big time. But what most didn't realise is that it took me five years to become an 'overnight' success. So for people who are reading this thinking, 'I've been to so many conferences, I've read so many books, I've done so many different courses on how to start business or how to do something on the internet', I say look at other people. You always see stories about successful people, and it's really tempting to look at yourself and think, 'I can't do it' and 'Obviously these other people are just smarter', but usually these people have spent quite a few years just learning and getting exposed to as many different ideas as possible.

"You need to choose an idea that suits your personality. Let me take you back to those years before I launched Wonderful Web Women, so you can appreciate how hard it was and so that you don't give up if you're at that stage now. I was a nurse. I had been a nurse for years and I was working at a university teaching other nurses when I fell pregnant with my first child. After my daughter was born I didn't want to go back to the hospital and I didn't want to go back to doing shift work. I didn't want to be around sickness in case I brought something home. So I decided to find an alternative, something that would allow me to stay at home but still

> **66 You need to choose an idea that suits your personality. 99**

gave me the intellectual stimulation that I needed. I'd heard from other people that you could make money on the internet, so I decided that that was what I was going to do. I decided to start an online business around something that I absolutely love: art. "

With no business, technical experience and another baby, Janet persevered with her plan to provide an online place for artists to display their work. This is how it happened.

Learning curve

"To keep me sane, when my babies were young, I studied art at my local college. In Australia at that time it was very difficult to find anywhere to display your art; there were only a couple of galleries in my town so not many people got to see your work if you were an artist. But there were a lot of fantastic artists, so I decided to start an internet art gallery. I've never worked in the art industry, was only capable of checking my email, knew nothing about websites and had never run a business, but I still went ahead. Needless to say, there was a humongous learning curve. I did every free course that I could find on how to set up a business and really just learned the hard way.

"I met someone at a party who said they could create a website for me, but that was a mistake. Lesson number one: you get what you pay for! Nice person, but there was no incentive for them to keep on delivering. So that's another lesson I have learned; if there are things that you don't want to take the time to learn yourself, you need to outsource, but it's much better to use a professional. It'll be done so much faster and saves a lot of heartache. To cut a long story short, five years later, I had one of the largest internet art galleries in Australia,

❝ Lesson number one: you get what you pay for! ❞ representing artists from all around the country. We had thousands of works for sale and I had made the business profitable, but only just. ❞

While building up her art gallery business Janet was also putting time and money into learning more about the world of internet marketing. This knowledge actually led her to sell her original business and start up Wonderful Web Women, and this time Janet actually did some research and had a plan!

Finding the model that suits you

❝ I've now invested in my education, because after trying to do it all myself I realised that to make an impact I needed to learn how to market. In business the primary thing you have to do is be a marketer. I started going to internet conferences and at the very first one I went to I learned about information products. I had never heard of this concept before, even though I had actually purchased some. Essentially, instead of me selling one high-priced original artwork I could be creating one information product, which could be an eBook, audio CD or boxset containing information that people wanted, that I could then sell over and over and over again. I remember going to these conferences and thinking, 'What am I doing? I'm working so hard selling these original artworks and I've spent a fortune setting up this really sophisticated website, yet everybody phones me because they want my reassurance that they are purchasing beautiful artwork'.

❝ My business wasn't giving me the life that I wanted so I came home from one conference, looked at my options and sold the gallery. I sold it for a song because I believed that keeping it was holding me back, so I didn't hold out to get the best price I could. I needed to get rid of it and move on, so I sold the art gallery for enough money to get myself new computers, new desks and everything I needed to set up a proper home office. The reason I tell that story is because I really want to get the message out that it's normal to take a while to learn all of these things and find the model that's best for you. There are so many models that work on the internet but the key is to find the one that suits your personality and your goals. "

Looking for role models

"That was the first part of my journey, and as a result of learning so much from internet conferences a lot of people started asking me if I would help them to get their business online. I was happy to help and was doing a lot of work for free until one night a friend said, 'Janet, why are you helping everybody for free? You should be charging for your knowledge. You have a business there'. This had never occurred to me. I guess you don't always value your knowledge when all you see is how much there is for you still to learn.

"I continued going to conferences but there was one thing about those events that got to me; you would go for four days, really really long days from 9 in the morning to 9 at night, and amazingly successful people would be on stage sharing what they knew – but 99% of them were men. There were no women up on the stage. It was really frustrating. And when everybody went out during the breaks and talked about speakers the big thing I was hearing from other women was, 'Where are our role models?' I needed to see successful women that were doing this. I couldn't relate to all that testosterone on the stage. There were no mothers up there. Surely people know that these guys probably had somebody else running the home and raising the family?

"That really got me thinking: If I can find some fantastic role models, as many different types of women as possible – mothers, grandmothers, highly educated, poorly educated, etc, who are a success on the internet,

66 In business the primary thing you have to do is be a marketer. 99

then surely women will be able to find someone who they can relate to? I wanted to showcase role models so women can think, 'She's just like me; if she can do it, then I can do it!' That thought kept going through my mind, so I started doing market research. "

Market research in the women's toilet

" I have found that market research is the one thing that everybody wants to cut short. I spent a year doing it. I knew before Wonderful Web Women that there was a demand for what I wanted to do. But when I ran my idea past my mentors, they said, 'It's not going to work because there aren't enough successful women out there. You're going to alienate half of the market because the men are going to think you're a man-hater and then a lot of the women will think that too so they won't want to be affiliated with you. Besides, women don't spend money so you won't make much from it'. Not that they were trying to criticise me! They were trying to give me advice about what they thought would be a good niche for me to go into, but because I had spent so much time talking to my target market, I knew that this is something they wanted.

" I did my market research by going online and finding out what sort of things people were searching for on Google. I was also reading forums and getting ideas about what people were talking about. But my best research was to go and seek out my target market. They hang out at internet-marketing conferences, so I turned into an internet-marketing conference junkie to ask them what their frustrations were. And do you know where I would find the greatest concentration of my target market? In the women's toilet! I know this sounds weird but I spent a lot of time at these conferences and during all of the breaks I'd stay in the loos. There's always a queue in the ladies, so what do you do? You talk to the people who are lining up. If you're at a conference you're talking about the speakers, and what you're learning, and what your biggest frustrations are. So that's what I did. I would stay in the women's toilet asking questions. Towards the end when I knew that I was definitely going to be building this business, I even took along my mp3 recorder, worked my way along the queue and asked people whether I could record their answers because I couldn't remember them all. I asked, 'What is your biggest frustration?' and 'If I can interview successful women, what do you want me to ask them?'

" I knew that even though people were advising me it wasn't going to work, I knew my target market and I knew this is something they wanted. So for that reason I felt confident about taking a big risk. That was when I decided not to take on any more customers who had started paying me to build their businesses. I refused all customers, but because I had success with people, I would still be getting phone calls a few times a week saying. 'Janet can I pay you thousands of dollars to set up my internet business?' and I (although it sounds unbelievable) was turning them away. "

Confident that she had a hot target market Janet went ahead with her plan to create Wonderful Web Women and used a strategy that has really paid off. Janet explains.

Choosing to do what scares me the most

" At this stage, the knowledge that I had was just from going to those internet-marketing conferences and from my online art gallery. To people who are thinking, 'I don't know enough to be able to consult and help other people', I say if you've been learning a lot of these strategies then you would know more than 90% of people out there, so you do have the skills to start a business helping others. I decided that I was going to concentrate on learning what I needed to do to launch Wonderful Web Women and then to set it up, and that's what I did. I made the decision sitting in one of those conferences. I remember being in the audience, looking up at the speakers on stage and thinking, 'Wow, they are so successful. What is different about them? Why have they created success? Why do they have confidence to get up there?' Then it just struck me. I thought, 'They probably weren't born this way, they are probably just normal people but at some stage they've made a decision to do something that really scared them, to have made such progress'.

"So I made a decision, sitting there in the audience, that from then on if I had a choice between two ways of doing something to get an outcome, one way tha kept me in my comfort zone and another way that scared me but had huge rewards, then I would choose to do what scared me! I've never done that before but it's not that risky because if a particular strategy is not going to work, the risk is actually that I'm not capable of doing it because it's something that I've not learned to do yet or requires the confidence I never had. So I made the decision that I would always choose the option that scares me. I made that commitment to myself and I've kept it.

"When it came to launching Wonderful Web Women, I knew that I could either help others to grow their businesses, encourage them to put themselves out there and be the face of their business, or I could concentrate on growing my own brand with me being the face of the business; the latter scared me so I had to do it. I really wanted to find amazing success stories, however, I'd never interviewed anybody before and knew nothing about recording technology. So with absolutely no experience but a lot of hope, I just went straight to the top to get the biggest names that I could find. That really, really scared me so I knew that's what I had to do. Thankfully they all said yes.

"When people came to my website and saw I was interviewing these really successful women they thought that obviously this person, this Janet Beckers, must be reputable if other people are endorsing her. As a consequence I haven't had to go looking for anybody to interview since. They have either come directly to me or been referred. By starting with the biggest names first, I set the benchmark. That was a really important decision to make, and the only reason I made it is because it scared me."

The business model that Janet started with is actually very simple. She built an online community of members through her website, then interviewed experts in her field to teach success strategies to her members. A lack of experience and no contacts didn't stop Janet, and things turned out well. Plus it proved to be a great benefit to her members, as Janet explains:

Building the community

"I liked interviewing because I wasn't Janet being the expert, I was Janet being the reporter on a journey of her own and sharing it with other people. It wasn't me setting myself up as the leader because I didn't think I was one at that stage. After my first tele-seminar interview I thought, 'I could open up the conference call to all the listeners so people can talk and I can find out what everybody's thinking, what they're doing and why they would want to invest in my paid membership'. Initially I felt vulnerable, having people live on the line, and some wanted to talk to me rather than the expert! It was a really good idea because people wanted to talk and some actually created relationships from that very first call and ended up doing business together. So now every time I do an interview I open up the lines for an hour afterwards and people talk and ask questions and I can give answers or other people on the call can contribute.

"As a result, Wonderful Web Women has really grown into a community; it's not just about me, and that's incredibly satisfying for both me and my members. It gives them confidence because sometimes their role model isn't the person I've interviewed, it's another person who is also on their own path but has success in a different area. Sometimes people relate to somebody who is at the same level as them but moving out of their comfort zone. My intention was always for people to find role models and that's what has happened. Only you know what your comfort zone is. The things I've found scary some people might have coped with easily and for other people they might be so terrifying that they wouldn't have even considered doing it, but that's okay."

Janet moved quickly from doing it all herself to outsourcing support, and as a result of growing her business she has gained pleasure from being able to pay other mums working from home:

Creating opportunities for other mothers

"You know what your level of confidence is at each stage, so decide to do the thing that scares you the most, because every time you do it and you succeed you get that little bit more confident. As a consequence Wonderful Web Women has grown really fast; we built it up to a six-figure business incredibly quickly and it continues to grow. We've recently taken on two more staff so that brings us up to a team of seven people working from their homes around the world. The majority of them are mothers and I find it incredibly satisfying that not only am I a mother running a business from home but I've been able to create opportunities for other mothers to be able to work in the same way and contribute to our business. It starts by taking that first step and making that first decision, then your decisions get bigger and bigger and bigger. I'm planning things that I wouldn't have even dreamt of doing two years ago. It's been the incremental challenges that have allowed me to think so much bigger."

Janet and I share a similar vision to support women in business, specifically online businesses, and to build a community, giving them a peer group to belong to. I think it's important that as the leader of the community you understand your people. You know most of the problems they are facing and you know what makes them tick. Janet is now in a strong position to coach others, having been through the start-up process and built a successful business.

> **❝ It starts by taking that first step and making that first decision. ❞**

Discipline not distraction

❝When people first come to me they always ask, 'Where do I start?', and I tell them that they need to find a way of working that suits their personality. I've tried a few techniques that could be done by anyone as long as they followed the steps. It was really impersonal stuff to do with Google AdWords and selling eBooks on topics that you didn't really care about, but there is a demand for it. I've got a couple of those projects that still run, but I could never keep up the energy because I've never been passionate about them. I find that most people have a song in their heart and want to share it with the world, and if you can tap into what that song is and build your business around it, you will have the momentum to keep on going up all the inevitable hills. In any business there are going to be times when you come up against a brick wall and feel like you're bashing your head against it, but if you've got passion and drive then you'll realise that you can jump over it. My passion is stories, I love people's stories. So for people who are just starting out, I say you really need to build your business around your passion.

❝I used to think that people needed to work out what their passion was, but I've realised that entrepreneurs are passionate about so many things that the problem is choosing which of those to concentrate on and having the discipline to ignore the others. That's where Bright Shiny Object Syndrome comes in. It takes a lot to choose and that's what makes entrepreneurs such interesting people to be around. I write down all my ideas in the front of my diary, and then I close it, because if I start doing them I get distracted from the one thing I've chosen to concentrate on at that moment. It takes a lot of discipline.❞

So, once you've stopped yourself getting distracted by every bright idea you come up with, you need to find out if there is a demand for what you are planning to do. Don't convince yourself that everyone's going to want what you've got; instead spend time on research before you spend any more time and money. Here is Janet's advice on choosing the right business:

Looking for demand and competition

"You need to work out the niche you are particularly interested in and some people find this really tough. Try to work out which one is going to keep you motivated the longest. There has to be a demand in your niche for you to know there is a target market. Do your research. Search Google. E.g. for something to do with art, search for artists' names or oil paintings and print making to see the websites that are already available. Check if there are people advertising on Google's results pages, but also bear in mind that if you find a niche where nobody is advertising then it may be because nobody's interested. So competition is actually a good thing. Spend some time hanging out in forums and do not rush this part because if you build a business where there's no demand, it's going to break your heart and probably put you off trying any other ideas.

"I suggest people start with a blog. It's so easy to get one up and running. A blog gets you writing, getting things out of your own head and shared with the world. You should write really short articles of about 400 words on your chosen topic. The beauty of this is, firstly, it helps you get your thoughts together and you're actually taking some action by writing about your topic; and secondly, it helps you understand what it is that you need to offer in that area. The added bonus is that search engines like Google absolutely love blogs, so while you're writing you're actually building

> **" You really need to build your business around your passion. "**

up your ranking and after a while people who are searching on certain key words will find you. "

" Do your research. "

Having decided on the right niche for your business you now need to start attracting clients. Your first few may be people you already know or those from your local area, but if you are serious about building an online business then you'll need to start getting your website to work for you. A quick and easy way to start attracting prospective clients is to offer some free information from your website in return for the visitor's name and email address. You could start with a simple email newsletter, which gives you the opportunity to keep in regular contact with your list of prospective clients. Janet talks further about the importance of building a client list:

Building a list

" Once people start to interact with you, you then have an opportunity to build a relationship. Having started your blog, the next most important thing is to collect the email addresses of people who visit your website and build up a list, because only about 1% of visitors will ever buy anything (and you don't have anything to sell yet anyway because you don't know what solutions people need). So for the 99% of people that never intend to come back to your website, you need a way to obtain their email address. It's not usually enough to say 'receive my newsletter', because people get far too many emails and are selective about who they give their address to. You need to have something that you can give away via your website that will entice people to join your mailing list. It should be something that people who are interested in your topic would want, so if you blog about yoga don't give away something on marketing strategies!

" Collecting email addresses and giving something for free is how you progress from a blog to building a list. If you're asking people to sign up then you have got to build a relationship, so the things I give away I could just as easily sell. Give away really good stuff, otherwise people aren't going to expect to learn from you. Then you can ask your subscribers what they want. If you know what their problems are you can give them a solution, and if they'll pay you to provide solutions then you've got yourself a business.

"Now that you've got the two essential tools – a blog and an email list – and people have told you what their problems are, your job is to convince them that you're the one that can solve them. That's when you start writing articles on your blog answering specific questions – you need to demonstrate that you are an expert. And that's how also you continuously build on your traffic.

"This is how to build up a business slowly if you don't know where to start, but these techniques are also going to build a business that is going to last. It's so important to keep in touch. These days there is so much communication and so many things that are vying for people's attention that if you're not getting in contact with people at least once a week those people are going to forget who you are. You want to be fresh in their mind when they're ready to buy.

"Another key is the 80/20 rule. I run my life by this and it's probably the biggest lesson I learned in business. You don't have to be 100% perfect, but if you can, get it 80% perfect. It's the same rule that states 80% of your money will come from 20% of your customers. I even do the same in my communication; I give 80% free content and spend 20% of my time selling. In my ezine I will write an article, I'll put in a titbit, I'll recommend resources and I'll promote one product. Because of that people don't feel pressurised. At one event I did I gave 100% free content and didn't have anything to sell, but people came up to the saying they were upset that they didn't have the opportunity to buy from me. That was a big lesson. How can they continue to do business with you if they like what you do and you're giving a great service solving their problems but you have no further resources for them?"

> **"** If you're not getting in contact with people at least once a week those people are going to forget who you are. **"**

Relationships equal cash

"Encourage a two-way relationship because customers want to buy from those they know and trust. Ask questions in your emails and in your blog to encourage feedback. Allowing that relationship to happen gives people a feeling that they're not just being talked at they're also being listened to. Find as many opportunities as you can to give those people on your list a chance to tell you what's on their mind. These strategies will help you to build a business that is going to last, especially if you're just starting out and don't know where to go. The most important thing is relationships, and in any business, especially on the internet, relationships equal cash. So the more relationships you can build, the stronger your business is going to be. The web can actually help you be more personal and that should be your focus when you're building your business."

Janet's business is a great example of how you could start an information-based business and build a community of members from scratch. By giving women a place to visit online and filling it full of valuable content, including audio recordings of all her expert interviews, Janet has been able to build, a business she is passionate about and help many other women start and grow their businesses too. It's a really simple business model and this is how Janet describes it:

Providing solutions

"I make money by finding out what people's problems are and helping to solve them. I did that initially by going to conferences, but I built on it through surveys and talking to people during the times that I opened the telephone lines, so I know what the problems in my market are. I solved those problems and made money in a variety of ways. One of them is through the Wonderful Web Women membership. Members pay a monthly fee so I know that every month there is going to be a certain amount of money coming in, and as long as I keep my membership at a certain level I can always pay my business expenses. Hence I love a continuity programme, which is where people are committing to pay for a certain number of months so you always know how many months someone will be paying membership fees. We've recently had our second birthday I just looked at our database and we've got members who have been with us for two years, 24 payments so far, and we're giving recognition to those members because they can start contributing to our community.

"I'm also selling $2000 packages that show people how to replicate what I've done, which includes videos, checklists, templates, and audio classes. People can apply these in their own niche. I also do one-to-one coaching. Another way we make money, and this is a great way for people to start out, is as an affiliate. Once you know what people's problems are, you don't necessarily have to be the person who makes the product that solves their problem – instead, find someone who has already made a great product, join them as an affiliate and then promote their product to your people."

The technology is out there to help you build a similar business to Janet's; all you need to do is decide what information you could base your business around. What problem can you help to solve by providing the answers, either yourself or through industry experts? I can really relate to much of what Janet is doing and through Supermummy I have created a social network for mumpreneurs, a membership site and provided a step-by-step guide to help mums start a social-network business from home. I know that online communities continue to spring up, and following the phenomenal growth of social networking sites like Facebook I believe that we will see many more niche social networks and membership sites based in the UK as the awareness increases. Needing to belong to a group or community is important to most people, so could creating an online community be for you? Have a think about it while you read through the rest of the book.

MEET ELIZABETH POTTS WEINSTEIN

"CREATING AN INTERNET EMPIRE WITH A TODDLER UNDERFOOT"

Elizabeth Potts Weinstein is a mumpreneur who helps other small business owners 'live their truth', which she defines as building a business with integrity, passion and authenticity that also makes money. You can read her blog and find out more about her project and coaching programme at www.elizabethpottsweinstein.com. She's also the founder and editor-in-chief of *The Wealth Spa* online magazine, (now closed), an attorney and certified financial planner by training, a speaker, author of *Grow Up! Strategies*, coach, blogger, radio-show host and mum to four-year-old daughter Grace. Phew!

Elizabeth has been in business for six years and recently posted a video on her blog titled 'Confessions of Unprofitability' revealing that she has invested all profits back into the business as a strategy for building long-term growth. This also means that she has not yet paid herself, so how can she be a millionaire mumpreneur? Read Elizabeth's blog and you will see how passionate she is about her business and that she has certainly helped others to achieve great results in their businesses, yet she openly admits to not taking any money out of her company. She shows great humility and vulnerability by telling the truth about her journey and finds strength in focusing on who she needs to be each day and living in the moment instead of thinking about how much money she wants to make. Like all the mumpreneurs in this book, Elizabeth has built a virtual business and I wanted to share her story with you to give you a variety of real-life stories. It all comes down to your personal definition of success, as it can be measured in so many ways. Elizabeth goes from strength to strength in making a true connection with her community, bringing value to others through her business and she loves what she's doing. Maybe that is worth a million? Let's find out how she went from being an attorney to coaching others to 'live their truth'. Elizabeth takes us back to the early days:

ELIZABETH'S STORY

"I graduated from law school and went to work for a giant law firm. I actually worked at a couple of different firms, mostly because I didn't really know what to do but I did well enough in law school that I could get those jobs. After a couple of years I realised that it wasn't a good fit for me. There were things I liked about it, but I wanted to have clients who were people rather than corporations and to have more flexibility in my working day. One of the things that I really wanted to have was more joy and passion about it.

"I left a big firm and opened my own business. At first, I didn't really know all of the different options out there for having a business, so I was doing financial consulting and legal work. I was meeting clients and charging by the hour. It was just like what I did in the law firm except the clients were individuals and small-business owners as opposed to gigantic corporations. During this time, my daughter Grace was born so we employed a part-time nanny so that I could continue to see clients and work on my business."

Elizabeth took the usual path of becoming self-employed by doing the same role as when she was an employee. The reality, however, of being self-employed is the challenge of marketing yourself, getting enough customers on a regular basis and doing your own administration. Elizabeth explains how it worked out for her.

Disillusioned and bored

"I was becoming really disillusioned and bored with my business. I hated leaving my daughter, and I felt like I was leaving her more and more. I needed more and more hours because I was seeing more and more clients. I've now changed my business to match the lifestyle that I want to have and to fit it better into my life. It meant I wouldn't have as much face-to-face time with clients, but I could still teach the things

I enjoy teaching, and help a lot of business owners and individuals. I could do it, for the most part, with my daughter in the room and with minimal childcare needs. When I first started up I had a website, but fundamentally my business was service-based. I did financial and estate planning for individuals so I would meet people and charge by the hour for the work that I did for them. The only online presence that I had was the site and I would get enquiries that way, but it was really just brochureware for people who had the information already."

How did Elizabeth make the transition from seeing clients face-to-face to offering a virtual service instead?

Doing a better job with the website

"After I had my daughter I really wanted to work less hours, because as you can imagine you can't see clients face-to-face with a child in the room. I also wanted to limit the amount of time I physically spent with clients, and there was a lot that I could do online with my daughter in the room so I wanted to pursue that. I started by figuring out how I could do more with the website and use it to bring in leads and prospects. By doing a lot more online, once I'm actually talking to people on the phone or seeing them one-to-one they're already clients and they're paying me, so I don't have to do much free face-to-face work.

"I evolved as I started leveraging my time. Instead of just working with clients face-to-face, I wanted to serve people in a different way. That's when I started to create information products that people can buy online. I use the site to bring in leads as well as sell products. I make money without having to be there in person. A lot of it was motivated by wanting to be with my daughter more and to only require a very small amount of childcare. It wasn't a smooth process though and all of this has taken up the last five years."

A key advantage of having a website as your business is the ability to quickly update and adapt it. When analysing your business, focus on your website; not just the design, look at whether it's actually doing a good job of collecting leads and converting those leads into paying customers. Remember, the easy way to do this is by simply adding a basic form to your website where your visitors can sign up for your free email newsletter, eBook or whatever it is you want to distribute. Elizabeth shares how she learned many ways to improve the website she already had in place:

Re-launch the entire website

"I had a website that my existing clients loved but it didn't get any traffic. When I launched my ezine it was just a few new clients that were signing up and I didn't really bring in any leads that year. There were so many things I didn't know about producing an ezine and my first edition was really just a long article. It was very intellectual and in-depth, took me forever to write and became a really tedious task. I would put it out once a month or sometimes alternate months, whenever I could find the time to write these great long pieces! Eventually I went to a workshop and I learned that I was doing a lot of things wrong! I learned how to do an ezine, how to give away a special report and how to generate different items, such as information-based products.

"I decided to re-launch my entire website and completely changed it. Before, it was like a brochure and it was all about me. I radically altered it and I launched *The Wealth Spa*, with both sites then being content-oriented. *The Wealth Spa* is technically a blog but I call it a magazine because of its complexity. It has tons of free content and that's also how I get traffic, because a lot of people find it when they Google something – I think this is the best kind of traffic you can get. But it takes time to build that up. I learned tips and tricks from other internet marketers to help my search result listings. When people come to my website some of them sign up for the ezine and return frequently. I have actually re-launched *The Wealth Spa* three times in the last three years because I am constantly learning."

You now have a better understanding of how it's possible to switch from a one-to-one customer model to going virtual. But how do you know it will work? How do you decide what kind of product or programme to develop and launch? The truth is, you simply won't know for sure unless you test it. Elizabeth shares some of her experiences of testing different ideas within her business.

Experimentation

"I actually don't do one-on-one consulting for financial planning and estate planning anymore. I decided to concentrate on my new strategy instead, so I had to change my website accordingly. That's how it has evolved over the last couple of years. There have been a number of things that I've launched that simply didn't work. I thought about doing a continuity programme, which is a membership-based service where I would coach a group during a set period and set a schedule. I was doing that for financial planning, launched it, but only a couple of people signed up – and they were already clients! It just didn't slide for that market and for that target audience, so after a while I decided to cancel it.

"It's important for people to understand that this is incredibly common. I heard an interview with a very prominent internet marketer who said that out of every ten programmes he launches, eight of them fail. Those remaining two make a lot of money, or one of them does, but *8* of them fail. And that's really hard for people to get – me included. I would say at least half, if not 75%, of everything I've launched does not make money so you have to launch a good range.

"I also do a lot of experimentation, especially with the website. It's one of the things that's hard in the beginning because what you don't realise is that when you see people who are an 'overnight' success, especially those who make millions of dollars, they've been working at it for years; you just see the end of the process.

" For me it's about doing things that I feel are congruent. I launched a lot of products because someone told me to. Maybe a friend, a colleague or a coach I worked with, someone said 'You should do this' and it would be something that looked good on paper but I was just not feeling it. Yet I did it anyway – and they all flopped. The things that I know are right are the things that work, but what works for me won't necessarily work for you. You have to do something that fits within your business. "

Read Elizabeth's blog (www.elizabethpottsweinstein.com) and you'll soon discover that she is passionate about speaking the truth, in both her personal and business life, and her business has taken a new direction in encouraging others to 'live their truth' in business, meaning to build a business with integrity, passion and authenticity. She explains this in more detail:

Developing a business around your passion

" You may be passionate about marketing, or love spirituality, or pets, or food; whatever your passion is, think about developing a business around it.

" You need to think about what you want your days to be like. Who do you want to be working with? Where are you going to be doing this? What will you be doing during the day? What hours do you want to work? And I don't just mean how many hours in a day, but do you want to work 9am to 5pm, or in the morning before the kids wake up and in the evening after they go to bed, or while they're at school? Do you want to travel or not?

" All of these things affect the kind of business you want. You can take your passion and create 100 different business types. This is something to be really conscious about when starting out or morphing your business into something that's a better fit. Maybe you would style it the same way, or use some of the same technology, but it will

> " Whatever your passion is, think about developing a business around it. "

need to be customised. Your passion is what's going to come across. You'll always sell it better because you'll be speaking about something you're passionate about, and people are going to resonate with that. You're also going to work a lot harder at it because you'll love what you're doing. It takes a lot of time. It may be time when your child(ren) can be in the room with you, but it's still a lot of your time and energy. The more personal I get and the closer I'm involved the better the end result. It happens over and over again."

How has Elizabeth's business, *The Wealth Spa*, evolved from financial advice to helping people transform their hobbies into businesses? Elizabeth calls it 'finding your truth; so let's learn more about that.

A holistic evolution

"In the beginning I was giving people financial and estate planning advice as an attorney. I don't have a degree in marketing or coaching but all of those things are naturally integrated in your own business. One of the things I talk about is holistic wealth; it's also about holistically helping people because all of these things are interrelated. Transforming your hobby into a business means that you need to know about some technical stuff, financial and legal things and marketing, but a lot of it is about mindset and a lot of it is about passion. If you do just one piece at a time it's not going to happen; it's when you get all the pieces together that you have the breakthrough and the overnight success. My business has been through a huge evolution in the last six years. Previously, I was always waiting for something to happen before I would consider myself successful, such as having a

> **❝** If you do just one piece at a time it's not going to happen; it's when you get all the pieces together that you have the breakthrough and the overnight success. **❞**

certain number of clients or a certain amount of money. I came to a point where I said, 'I'm not going to sit and wait for anything to happen anymore', because at that time my daughter was in daycare four days a week and I really wanted to home-school her but I was waiting for *something* to happen before I did that.

"It actually took a couple months to get my act together but a big thing for me is feeling successful on a daily basis and enjoying what's going on; even the things that fail or that aren't making money yet. Nothing's sat waiting for us; it's about creating a life that you want today. Success will come faster when you're feeling that way, but you're also going to enjoy your daily life so much more. When you're trying to be an entrepreneur and a mum all at the same time it's so easy to feel like you're not being good at either. You feel like you're failing at everything, and being pulled in many directions. I deal with it by simply being in the moment of that day."

Elizabeth's business has even given her the flexibility to home-school her daughter. Interesting. Living, working and schooling at home? Good luck Elizabeth! She talks about how 'living in the moment' works for her and I can see how this could be a great coping strategy, especially on those days when it's easy to procrastinate because you are worrying about your huge to-do list. It comes down to mindset so in what other ways has Elizabeth's thinking changed since becoming a mumpreneur?

Test the water

"I think in a very different way now about launching products and I launch things differently. I don't put my eggs in one basket. I trial things and find out if anybody is interested in it. If everybody is keen then I'll put all my money and time into it and do a full version. To give you an example, I'm thinking of doing a live event but I'm not going to sign a contract with a hotel and spend a lot of money upfront. What I'm going to do is see if anybody wants to buy a ticket; if I sell a few tickets I'll hire a small place, and if I sell lots of tickets I'll get a bigger place. Knowing that some stuff isn't going to work means that now I spend money and invest time and energy in a different way. I test things first, and I expect that a certain percentage of things I launch are not going to click. So I have a different mindset now."

Always getting to the next level

"A mindset shift that's really important is to break out of being comfortable with a mediocre level of success. You can be safe and make a small amount of money, but you're never going to push the boundaries. I need to be doing something uncomfortable on a regular basis, almost everyday; if I get to a point where I reach a plateau and things start to become comfortable then I plateau in all areas of my business and I don't make any more money. I won't be selling any more products and everything starts to get boring. I remember doing the first day of my radio show and I was sick for a whole day as it was so nerve-wracking, whereas now I can just talk for an hour without any preparation. It's no big deal because I'm used to it. So it's always about getting to the next level. I used to be uncomfortable asking people to introduce me to someone, but I forced myself to do it and of course people were happy to, so I'm getting used to that and asking people, 'Hey can you introduce me to so and so?' Now I wonder why I was so scared because it's actually not a big deal."

Just like Karen and Janet, Elizabeth is also comfortable being uncomfortable and recognises that this as an effective way to keep making progress. She shares some more insights about that:

The most risk has the most reward

"I find that thinking this way is actually a self-protection mechanism. I find the things that make me the most uncomfortable are the ones that I need to do in order to get what I want, and which will make me successful. If there are ten things on your desk, tackling the one that makes you feel the most uncomfortable is the one you need to do or try first. Something inside you knows that the task with the most risk also offers the most reward. I think it's doing it on a regular basis too. I have something that I read to myself everyday that says, 'What could I do today that will make me uncomfortable?' and I make sure that there's something on my to-do list that takes me out of my comfort zone, even if it's something as small as sending an email or making one phone call that's a bit scary. Doing that on a regular basis will you get used to it, and take you where you want to be, faster."

Considering Elizabeth's background and experience I wonder what she thinks about the feasibility of starting a business in a difficult economy? Could it be seen as irresponsible or is it more irresponsible to give our time and energy to an employer and hope that they will in turn provide us with what we want? Elizabeth says:

Starting at the bottom?

"When everything's at the bottom there's the most up potential. A lot of people aren't going to start businesses and a lot of people's businesses have gone under. If you're going to be the person who can make it, you're going to get those clients and you're going to make those sales. An online business is the least expensive kind that you can start; of course you have to have a computer but you don't have large overheads and you don't require office space. There are many ways to be really lean and very conservative about how you spend your money because you don't have to spend much. You can even start off part-time, in the evenings and at weekends, if you need a steady job to pay the mortgage or rent. Because most businesses don't make money in the beginning you need to have some way to start earning quickly or you need money in the bank to pay your bills in due term.

" I can also guarantee that no matter what business you start or what the economy is doing, there will be naysayers in your life who will say, 'Who do you think you are?' but it's important to understand that some of them are saying that to protect you. They are saying it out of love because they don't want you to start a business, fail and get hurt. Other people are saying it because they don't have the guts to go for it themselves and if you go ahead and are successful, that means they could have done it too but didn't. Then they're confronted with their own feelings of failure."

It's tough when you don't feel supported, especially by friends and family, so I wonder whether Elizabeth gets enough support. If so, from whom? She tells us about the significance of finding a community to belong to:

Find people as crazy as you are

" An important thing is to find a community of like-minded people, who are as crazy (in a good way!) as you are. It could be a local group of other women, or other entrepreneurs who you meet up with once a week for coffee, or it could be an online programme that you're in. I'm in a mastermind group that meets a couple of times a year. It's for women who are entrepreneurs and they have all kinds of businesses. It's really important because these are all people who think that it's not crazy to have a business and who may have written a book or been on TV. All those things are normal to us, so we can talk about that and also be realistic about the things that fail because you need people to support you.

"One of my other big communities is on Twitter; there is an amazing community of people there who support me in what I'm doing. The people on Twitter who I speak to are very much like me. Both my mastermind group and my Twitter friends are all people who live in other states, and even other countries. It's sometimes hard to find someone nearby who's like you and understands what you are doing, but you can easily find someone in a different country that can be your friend and supporter. That's the amazing part of the internet; you don't even have to be in a remotely compatible time-zone to get support from another like-minded person. "

As well as business supporters, we all need other mums to share the joys and challenges of parenting, and the issue of choosing to work or stay at home is a hot topic. Being a work-from-home mumpreneur, has Elizabeth found fellow mums in her local community who are understanding and supportive of her choice?

Over-achieving mums

"Where I live, mums are very high achieving. We have two groups; one is the working mothers who have a full-time career, and here in the Silicon Valley that means working 60 hours a week, and they have a full-time live-in nanny if they have a small child or a part-time nanny if the child goes to school all day. The other group are mums who stay home with their children, and they can be over-achieving mums too. They have a bunch of different play groups, they have four children because you can't have one. If you're going to stay home you have to have four! They take up different groups, they have all these commitments, they're volunteering and they're very active. Because they used to have very over-achieving corporate jobs, now they're at home they're 100% into it.

" I travel in both worlds because I have my own business but I only use four to six hours of childcare a week, so people don't know what category to put me in. It's isolating in a sense as people don't tend to understand unless they're familiar with it. There's a lot of negativity in the working mum vs. stay-at-home mum debate, and I'm in both and neither group in a lot of ways, so it can be very strange.

" One of the reasons I look for other women who have their own home business, or have an office but they're home a lot with their child, is so I can meet with other people who understand what I'm doing; it's like we're in our own third group. You have to find other people who are like you. Sometimes when I'm with other mums I don't talk about what I do because it's just like opening a can of worms, so I just say, 'I'm home with my daughter' and I don't explain further. It's a bit like talking about politics or religion. I won't debate it because what you do is your own choice and you do what is right for you and your family.

" Most of the people I've been friends with for a long time still don't understand what I do. They'll hook up with me on Facebook and ask, 'What is all this stuff that you're doing?' So I have new friends, like the people in my mastermind group. We've spun off on our own, and we're still meeting regularly. They are like-minded entrepreneurs. That's something everyone needs, whether you pay to be in a group or just naturally find a group of people. You need to have others who understand what you're talking about and the vision you have for your business. "

I'm amazed (and very impressed) that Elizabeth has scheduled her business to the extent that she requires only four to six hours of childcare per week and is home-schooling her daughter. What does a normal day look like for Elizabeth?

Matching the flow of the family

"I work early in the morning or late in the evening and on the weekends, I have this bizarre crazy schedule. I don't have a normal day so I have a whole bunch of different ways for me to get work done. Part of it is working on things that match the flow of our family when my daughter doesn't need me. Happiness is enjoying the moment, whatever that moment is. Sometimes it is complete craziness and bad things are happening. It's really easy, especially as mumpreneurs because we're so insanely busy, to forget to appreciate our kids and spend those amazing moments with them. It may only be a split second moment with them. We don't always get to appreciate the cool things going on in our businesses because we're always looking for the next thing. A lot of happiness is about not looking for something to happen to make you happy but being happy with where you are. Of course we still want to have goals and move forward, but be happy where you are in this moment right now."

Elizabeth's certainly has a busy schedule, but rather than having a team of people supporting her she manages with a minimal amount. She explains further:

Growing virtually

"I have a virtual assistant who answers my phone and some of my emails. I also have a business with my sister who is a graphic and web designer and I'm a client of hers, and I outsource individual, specific projects like transcriptions. I have friends who run big companies that make millions of dollars yet have no employees (in the traditional sense). Instead they have 20 people who work for them from their own homes in different parts of North America. You can get very big and still be completely virtual. Eventually you may need to hire people but if you're making a million dollars you can easily afford them. When you're little you can grow virtually for a very long time. It's also a great way to keep your overheads low and run your business in a responsible way. You don't need employees because you can do everything virtually for a very long time and be successful. There are going to be days when your kid is sick, and you just have to say, 'The business isn't going to happen today'.

"There are going to be these temporary imbalances. You're never going to be able to do everything all at once. That was really interesting for me to learn. On the days when Gracie gets sick, I'm the one taking care of her, and nothing gets done. I just accept the fact."

Elizabeth has become very adept at working during short blasts of time in her day rather than taking a whole day to work on her business. I can relate to that as even though I am really productive during a few hours of uninterrupted time, I've also got loads done by consistently putting in 10-20 minutes here and there. But, I really must get the hang of scheduling time for myself as Elizabeth recommends:

Make time for yourself

"Part of the process is changing our insane perfectionist expectations and making some compromises. There is some practical stuff. You have to schedule time for yourself, even if it's just 15 minutes of sitting down and reading a book. You have to set boundaries with family, friends, loved ones, spouses, your business and your clients about what you're not willing to do. But also remember that they'll figure it out. The clients will figure things out. Your staff will figure things out if you let them. Don't multitask; especially if you have dedicated childcare time or your kids are at school; schedule blocks of time when you can be super-intense and 100% focused.

"I have activities that I can do with Gracie in the room, such as checking   email,   posting

" You can get very big and still be completely virtual. "

something to my blog that I've already written, uploading a guest post and social networking. I don't need to be super-focused to be on Twitter! I separate that from things I need to do when she is occupied or being cared for, like when I'm writing a blog post, talking on the phone, doing something intense or writing a sales letter for a new product. I split those tasks so that when I have two hours to get stuff done, I'm doing the most important things during that time. Everything else can get done in the little pockets of time throughout the day.

" When I have this block of time, I do the most important thing first, unless it's a phone call or something that I have to do because of timeliness. I don't check my emails during this time. I have to catch myself though! I'm not even allowed to check Twitter. I just get that one thing done and cross it off. Then I can go on to the daily stuff, like blogging, sending out my latest ezine, answering emails, etc. I'll sit down and write in my journal, 'The most important thing I can do today is', and then not think. I let my hand write. Sometimes, some interesting things come out. It's intuitive. "

Elizabeth has been very frank about how she evolved her Wealth Spa business into her 'live your truth' project and programmes and how she has had to endure a great deal of trial and error. I'm interested to find out how she actually makes money:

Making the money

" My website has lots of free stuff and free downloads and now I have information products, e.g. the money tree system, plus I have my book and CDs on different topics that people can buy. I also regularly teach different coaching programmes. I do a group coaching programme, record it and turn it into an information product. I still do a little bit of one-to-one coaching with people, but I don't take on many clients because it takes a lot of mental energy for me to work with someone like that, and it's also one of the things that I need childcare for.

" I also have the graphic and web-design service business with my sister and I do a little bit of coaching with that. One of the big models for my business is offering products and services to my community that are things I don't necessarily do myself. I introduce services that people need whereby I have someone else who can provide that service but it's someone I'm overseeing. There's lot of ways you can do things that bring more value without necessarily taking up more of your time. "

As you've seen, Elizabeth's business has not only transformed from consulting with clients on a one-to-one basis to serving multiple clients through coaching programmes and information products, but over the years she has also changed her business. During this transition she has implemented many of the strategies that you are learning about, such as building a list of prospective clients, maintaining regular contact with her community, and creating virtual products and services.

Most new businesses need time to build up enough revenue to turn a profit, however Elizabeth has now been in business for over six years. Could it be that in finding her 'truth' and making a decision to align her business more to her values, she now has more passion than ever for her business and that is what will really make the difference? As her 'live your truth' project was only launched recently it's too early to tell, but in comparison to the other MMs stories it's evident that only Elizabeth has completely re-invented her business whereas the others have continued with the same core niche and target market. Elizabeth has been running her business in a similar way to the other MMs but how has she not achieved similar financial results? What's the difference? Could it be connected with Elizabeth wanting to find her own way and not necessarily follow 'the rules' of the internet marketers who have influenced her business in the past?

Any entrepreneur must be ready to adapt their business if things aren't working out and the reality is that Elizabeth has applied many virtual business strategies yet has not managed to make her business profitable

> 66 There's lot of ways you can do things that bring more value without necessarily taking up more of your time. 99

enough to pay herself, in effect making her a counter example of a MM. So, the truth is that yes it's possible that the same may happen in your business. In any business, actually, because there is never any guarantee of success, in profit terms, even if you are following a proven process or business model. Think of it as an entrepreneurial *X Factor*; I believe that what makes the difference is passion. Passion is the fuel that drives the entrepreneur.

On a positive note, the experience has helped Elizabeth to re-assess herself and her business and re-design it. It seems that it's only now that she is truly aligning both her passion and her skills and the 'live your truth' Project has launched successfully. Elizabeth still has a virtual business, she still leverages her knowledge through her coaching programmes and delivers her content using virtual methods like video and tele-coaching, but she is connecting and supporting her clients more than ever and leading a community and is more fulfilled.

MEET ALEXIS MARTIN NEELY

"THE INTREPID MUMPRENEUR"

ALEXIS'S STORY

Alexis Martin Neely is America's Favourite Lawyer®, the founder and CEO of the Family Wealth Planning Institute and is revolutionising the way legal services are provided to families and small business owners. She edits the online magazine *Family Wealth Secrets* (www.familywealthmatters.com) and is the author of *Wear Clean Underwear: A Fast, Fun, Friendly and Essential Guide to Legal Planning for Busy Parents.* On her blog (www.alexismartinneely.com) she describes herself as 'The Intrepid Mompreneur' and being a savvy, forward-thinking business woman, Alexis has built two million-dollar businesses (and sold one of them) while raising her two children.

Alexis's virtual business gives her the freedom to work from her home in California (though since our interview she has moved with her two children, her ex-husband, a dog, three cats, a snake and a turtle to Colorado!) be there more for her kids and maintain a long distance relationship with her boyfriend in Atlanta. She can plan her own schedule, which includes regular slots on TV as a legal commentator. It all sounds so exciting and inspirational but Alexis has been on a very personal journey to get this far, after she made the decision to burn the bridge and leave her job to go it alone. Alexis shares her story about how she got started.

Two new starts

"Back in 2000, I was working for a big law firm having graduated from law school in 1999 and done my year of clerkship. That year I also got married, got pregnant and had a baby! When I started out I was a mum and I had a stay-at-home husband. By 2003, we had two children. By then I had a six-figure salary but I was really unhappy. I stumbled upon a coach who helped me to see that I was never going to enjoy working for someone else and that I needed to go out on my own if I was really going to be happy in my life. I needed to create something completely different, something that I was going to be proud of and something that would allow me to really love my life and focus on my kids.

"In August 2003, I left the big firm and the big salary behind and started my own law firm. I was running that business until I sold it in 2008. I basically created a new business model in my law firm because when I first started up I didn't know anything about running a business or running a law firm, and over the next three years I proceeded to give myself a complete education in how to run a business.

"By 2006, I had grown my firm into a million-dollar business, but only by working crazy hours so I still wasn't getting to spend much time with my family. But by the end of 2006, I'd figured out how to run that business by working in the office two days a week and working the rest of the time from home. In 2007 I began to teach that method to other lawyers, then in 2008 I finally sold my business."

What's particularly interesting about the next part of Alexis's story is that she sold a very successful business with the intention of creating a new, completely virtual one. She has achieved similar results, but this time around it's on her terms. Let's find out more about that transition.

Going completely virtual

"I sold my bricks-and-mortar law firm so that I could work – do everything – completely from home with a virtual business. It's virtual but it's completely real and that business is now a million-dollar one. It's a movement that is changing the way families and small-business owners work with lawyers and the way lawyers work with families and small business owners throughout the United States and Canada. We're getting there and we're still just a couple of years old. We provide our services by phone, by email and through live events, but the key is I get to work from home every day, I get to decide my own schedule and I get to be here for my kids. This year we're actually home schooling them so that's a whole new experience. I think it's an entrepreneur's thing because we're rule breakers. We don't want to put our kids in a box. We want to turn our kids into little entrepreneurs and the school system is definitely not designed to do that. "

Making a bigger impact

" For me, going virtual was about how I could go from serving one client at a time to serving many people at a time. Did I want to provide my service or did I want to coach others in my industry to provide our service better? Let me explain that, because I think it's important for people to understand. I thought for a long time: how can I provide legal services virtually? There were ways that I could have done it. I wanted to make a big impact and I didn't want to continue to serve one-to-one. I decided that what I wanted to do is coach other lawyers in my industry on how to provide their service better. The other option would have been to convert my firm to a virtual one so that I could work with people without having to leave my home office.

" So there are two options when you're ready to take things to the next level. You can either figure out how to provide what you do virtually or how to coach others in your industry to do what you do. It's great to provide virtually because people are now very used to receiving training over the phone and online, through tele-seminars, tele-coaching programs, webinars, etc. "

We are certainly moving towards a world of virtual learning and even our education system is embracing this trend. If it's good enough for the Open University, it's good enough for us! Alexis expands on this point.

Apply it to your life

"It's important that people don't think, 'Oh, well that's fine for them because they're a university' or 'That's fine for them because they have this or that'. I didn't have anything. It was just me. I was a lawyer who felt stuck and I wasn't happy, and then I was stuck in a business where I had to leave my house and my kids six days a week to run it. I didn't feel like I could have the life I wanted. So I made a decision to do something different.

"I think the really important thing is that it's easy to say, 'Well, that can't work for me' or 'I'm different', but what you want to look for is how it can work for you and say to yourself, 'How can I apply this to my life? How can I hear what she's saying about what she did and apply it to my life?' That's where the transformation begins to happen. Write down your answer to that question. Get out a journal or even just a blank piece of paper and write the answers to the following: How can I do this in my life? How can I provide the service that I provide virtually from home? Who can I help? Who can I teach something to? What do I know that other people want to know? Then you'll begin to learn.

"People look at me, for example, and see that I've built two million-dollar businesses, but what they don't see is all the build-up to that point. Law school was three years of intense learning but after that there was another three years of intense investment in learning. I attended conferences both virtually and in person; I hired coaches and I read books. Reading is great, but the real transformation happens when after taking in that information you actually do something with it. So what can you do with that information? Never again read a book without saying, 'How can this change my life or someone else's?'

"I ask myself questions such as, 'How can this apply? How can I share this with the world? How can I help people with this information?' Because most people don't read and don't translate for themselves and if you can do that, if you can become a translator for people and really serve in that way, you can do it all from home, and get paid for it. It's the best way to be a mum. It was painful for me to be a mum when I had to work so much."

Alexis openly shares how her children have had a massive influence on her decisions and their influence on her decision to quit her job.

Needing to ask for help

"I remember one time I was working and my daughter was standing next to my computer, she must have been about six, and she's jumping up and down and trying to bother me. To me she was just being difficult, but my girlfriend happened to be sitting there and she said, 'Alexis, she wants you. She's really craving your attention right now. She wants your attention.' It was just like being slapped. I had to face what I didn't want to see, which was that my kids needed my attention and I was not able to give it to them. But that doesn't have to be the case, it just takes some time, and the sooner you start the sooner you're going to get to that point.

"Today it's different because I have so much help. When I was working in a big law firm I only had the support of my (now ex) husband. He was a stay-at-home dad and we did not have a housekeeper or a nanny; we did not have any other support. We did not even have any babysitters. We didn't have any family around. My mentality was that I had to do everything; it's the biggest false idea that I have ever had and that held me back the longest. As soon as I realised that not only could I not do it alone, but it really was complete ego to think that I could, that I needed help and I needed to ask for help, and I needed to be willing to pay for help, then everything shifted. It was hard for me, particularly as I grew up without money and without health insurance so there was a lot of financial fear in my family. I had to transcend that completely to be able to get the help that I needed."

How is Alexis's life different now, having created a situation where she can control her schedule?

Creating a community

"Today I have a virtual team of seven. I also have two people who help me here, from home. My best friend and her two kids live with us and she is doing the primary home schooling. We have another girlfriend that comes over who is home schooling her son and she does the home schooling of my kids too. There's a big network of support that I've created around myself. I've created this community because that's the answer to the future. That's really what we all want.

"I remember when I first moved here to Los Angeles; I had a baby and I had my husband but I didn't have any friends, I didn't have any family and I was so lonely. Heart-breakingly lonely. Every day was devastating just because I was so lonely and isolated. I didn't feel as if anybody understood what I was dealing with, and there was no one to talk to about it. I thought I wanted to have friends but what I realise now is that what I really wanted is what I have now. It's this community living and working together, where we all know that everybody is there to support each other. It's where everybody really gets to give their greatest gift and there's no judgment. There's a lot of acceptance, a lot of forgiveness, open communication, radical honesty and what's great is that that's getting passed on to the kids."

Let's not underestimate the power of community. Just think about how working from home, instead of being out for up to 60 hours a week, could connect you with your local community. Sometimes it's the most simple relationships, like getting to know everyone by name in your local shop,

> **66** My mentality was that I had to do everything; it's the biggest false idea that I have ever had and that held me back the longest. **99**

chatting with the other school-run parents and being involved in local events or attending local classes. Running a business from home also gives you the flexibility to choose who you want to spend your time with because you get the freedom to build your 'dream team' of people that you want to work with regularly. Alexis expands:

Your real life is your home life

"My kids are learning this by watching it happen and I think the key for every mumpreneur is to build yourself a community at work and at home. I love being on Twitter and Facebook because I want a community, but ultimately you realise that what's happening in your own home is your life. That's your life, your real life, and that's what's going to impact on your kids. If you're single and you don't have kids, fine, spend all your time online, but if you're a mum you also have to build your real-life community. In today's economic climate it's perfect.

"My best friend who lives with me now is able to do what she loves the most, which is taking care of our home, and I'm able to do the things that I'm passionate about. I love business and I love talking to people, inspiring people, and helping people to see different ways of thinking about things. Because my friend is willing to spend so much time with the kids meeting their needs, I'm able to work on my business and at the same time be meeting the kids' needs on a part-time basis."

As we talk, I can hear the conviction in Alexis's voice. She feels so strongly about creating community support in life and in business, and without an ounce of guilt for doing what she loves. It all seems a world away from the stressed-out lawyer she used to be. Alexis looks back at that time and shares how it affected her.

Your kids need your attention

"It was terrible. It felt horrible. My son would cry every single day when I left the house. He never wanted me to go. It was terribly painful and I had to find an alternative. I wanted to be able to meet his needs. What a lot of mums do, and believe me I was tempted, is they just pretend that there's something wrong with their child, saying that they are high-need, clingy or hyperactive. Your kids need you. It's part of their makeup, and maybe it's so that you will change your life. If you look at it that way and say, 'I'm going to go with that and see where it takes me', then you might find that you end up in a life that you absolutely love that looks nothing like you ever imagined."

Accepting the way things are

"I was so unhappy, but my coping mechanism at that time was to ignore that and try to control everything around me. I just kept trying to make things how I thought they should be, but things are always just the way that they are. The opportunity is to accept things the way that they are. For example, your child needs you. Maybe that's one of the ways things are. Or maybe you have one of those kids that is super easy and is happy when you drop them off at childcare, but that wasn't my kid. Maybe you know you are not meeting your own physical needs. You can feel that your body doesn't feel good. You know that it feels horrible and you feel like a big lump. Sunday comes along and all you want to do is watch TV and eat.

"I was there. I did all of those things. I just wanted to comfort myself and give myself a reward because I was working so hard and I was so unhappy, but the rewards were these things that weren't good for me. It was always short-term gratification, things like spending money or eating comfort food. They were never the things that really felt good, like exercising, which I hate to do, but I know that it feels really good when I do it. You begin to realise that when you start to take care of yourself. I never was able to do that when I was really miserable in my job. I say now that I was really miserable, but nobody would have ever known that at the time. I hid it very well. We're achievers and we want to be the best so we hide all those issues.

"Don't hide it anymore! Start to feel it, start to take care of yourself. I know you probably don't want to exercise, or get on the right eating plan, or look at your finances, because all that stuff takes time and you don't have any. I've experienced it but you just need to start with one thing and make a commitment to yourself. It finally hit me that this is not what I want for my life so I decided to go to a yoga class the next day. It sounds crazy but that class changed my life! It was as if my heart opened and all of a sudden I felt things that I hadn't felt in ten years, like joy and pleasure. I began to say, 'I want that, I want more of that, I want more out of life'. I think every mum wants more of that. The key is to find something you like. Ask yourself, 'What did I enjoy doing before I worked all the time?' "

Alexis has already accomplished so much and it seems like she has it all worked out, but she hasn't quite reached a place where she has a 'reasonable' schedule. I guess we all have a different definition of reasonable, but what's fundamental to growing any virtual business is having people working for you. Alexis explains how that's working out for her.

Having to push through

"I think there are probably a lot of mums who are already virtual and yet they're still working all the time. There are three stages: there's the mum that's still in the workplace who wants to get out; then there's the mum who's got out of the workplace and is now virtual but is working all the time; and the third level is the mum who's done it. She's figured out a way to be virtual and work a reasonable schedule. I would say that I'm still in that transition stage from two to three. The financial part of my life is great but there's still the time part of it.

"I recently had a nine-day vacation, but before that I was working absolutely insane hours, and it was terrible, and I knew it. But I couldn't do anything about it at the time, I just had to push through because I was in a growth period in my business. We had some really important things that had to happen and I had to power it out, but it was a great reminder of what I don't want.

"It requires a big investment of time and energy to make any transition, so know that during the transition periods you're going to be working the hardest. There are going to be times you want to give up but usually those times are right before the breakthrough, so if you choose to go back at that point then you'd be doing it at the worst possible point because you're losing all of the up side that you've spent all of this energy to gain. You're likely to experience that in each transition, but when you really understand why you're doing it, you can push through those periods, and you can ultimately realise what you want.

"We always have to come back to the question 'What do you want?' What energy do you want to cultivate in your life? What emotion do you want to make up the vast majority of your time? Is it feeling joy, connections, or is it feeling at peace? What is it? Then look at what energy you would give off if you had that? What feeling would you have if you had that in your life? How would others feel around you? Some people in your presence aren't going to feel good and that's a big thing to realise, especially for me because I like everybody to like me and I want everybody to feel good around me. Some people aren't going to feel good because you're shining the light on them not living up to their highest potential. So some people are not going to want to be around you, but that's okay."

I can understand why people might feel intimidated around a millionaire mumpreneur and look for ways to 'justify' their success in order to make themselves feel better. Having met Alexis and followed her for some time, the truth is that she is beautiful inside and out and you know what I think is really behind that million-plus turnover? Passion. It's not about the million *per se*, it's about the freedom and flexibility that financial freedom can give you:

Knowing what you really want

"You don't have to build a million-dollar business. You need to realise that it's about how much you are keeping in your pocket. You need to look at what you want from every level, and I don't think it should start with how much money you want to make. Start with what you want to experience in your life. Don't get so fixated on the million; it's the meaning that it gives you and what you can do with it."

When you can be true to yourself and see what you want your life to look like then you can plan your business to get you there.

Figuring out your gifts

"Start with the following questions: what energies do I want in my life? Do I want to be staying at the Four Seasons, the Motel 6, or am I fine with the Hilton? Do I want to have a big house or a small one? Do I want a lot of people living close to me?

"You can then begin to identify: how much do I need to make to have this life and support these things that I want? How am I going to do that in the least amount of time? Whatever your gift is, and we each have a gift, you just need to put a business model around it. The model is dependent on what you want to experience in your life. That's the process that I would take people through who are at that point of just starting out. All you ever need to know is the next step."

Alexis and I share big dreams and visions for our businesses and our lives. Sometimes the answer to what you really want scares you. It seems too big, too much, too far away to ever reach. Alexis reveals what happens when she sees the biggest and brightest visions for her business and her life:

"The thing that I really want the most is terrifying for me to talk about, and when I do I can feel tightness in my chest, because I don't want to say it and then not achieve it but it's only by saying it that you can get it. It's a catch-22 and you need to break through the conditioning and just let it out."

I wanted to introduce you to Alexis as I know there are plenty of mums on the 60-hours-a-week treadmill and she is a great role model for turning that situation around. Yes, she still works crazy hours sometimes, but now it's on her own terms for her own business. You can tell how much happier and fulfilled she is having taken control and created both a business and personal community that aligns with her values.

If you are in a similar situation can you see how you could go virtual? It may mean continuing to work with some clients on a one-to-one basis while you build up the virtual side of your business, but it is possible, as Alexis has proven, to do it your way. A lawyer that I know was recently made redundant and because her confidence was so crushed she was seriously considering 'party plan' in the evenings as her next option! With skills, talent and experience to offer why not get out there and do it differently, or better? Just like Alexis.

Fabienne Fredrickson is an amazing example of how a virtual business fits perfectly with family life. She has recently had her third child and is able to care for her newborn at home while still keeping her million-dollar business running smoothly. What's so interesting about the lifestyle Fabienne enjoys now is that she had it all planned before she was even married and had her first child! Knowing early on that she wanted a family and that her corporate career wouldn't give her the flexibility she wanted, she chose to make her own way.

Fabienne is the founder of Client Attraction (www.clientattraction.com), which teaches women how to consistently attract ideal high-paying clients, put their marketing on auto-pilot and create a million-dollar business while working less. She has made the seemingly impossible, possible. She's a mumpreneur who has exceeded the million-dollar mark without sacrificing her family life. Fabienne makes it all look so easy, but she has learned the hard way and earned her position from the focus and dedication she has shown and the systems and support she has put into place. So how did Fabienne get to where she is now?

FABIENNE'S STORY

"I spent 8 years in a corporate environment. I was good at my job, but then I became an advertising sales rep and I had people breathing down my neck and checking my every move. I had sales quotas and targets and I started feeling like I was in a prison. I was attending classes on nutrition in the evenings and at weekends and as I was feeling increasingly unfulfilled in my corporate job I felt the need to leave and start my own business. Both of my parents ended up being self-employed, so there was entrepreneurial spirit in my family. The defining moment for me was in 1999, when I quit my job and decided to take the great leap of faith and open up my own nutrition practice."

So Fabienne was a 'prisoner of work', only she created a great escape plan by studying nutrition in her spare time. Have you either considered or already started learning another skill in addition to your day job because *that's* what you're truly passionate about? Fabienne followed through and managed to make a success of her passion, but it wasn't an easy transition, as she explains.

Do or die

"One of my highest values, right up there next to family and having a yummy life, is freedom. I opened a private nutrition practice out of my home, which was a 300-square-foot apartment with a Murphy bed (I was single at the time). I had several clients and was making some money, good money by some people's standards, but my practice was definitely not full and even though my clients were getting really good results, I just didn't have enough of them to pay the rent. I was living on credit cards at the time and struggling to make $3000 a month, which wasn't covering my rent and my business. As you can imagine, the credit-card companies soon started calling wanting their money.

"I didn't know what to tell them so in time I stopped answering the phone, which is not very good for business, and then I started having what I now call the '3 am I don't have enough clients' sweats. I would toss and turn in the middle of the night unable to sleep several nights in a row thinking, 'What have I done? What am I going to do? I've got to find a way to get some clients'. As my corporate career had been in advertising, marketing and sales I assumed I would know how to do these things for my own business. I also thought that it would be a case of 'build it and they will come', but it wasn't that way at all. So once restless night I made a commitment to do whatever it took to fill my practice, get clients and make money. I took a no-excuses approach to finding out everything there was about attracting clients, networking, and closing the sale. And in doing so, I noticed that not everything that I wanted was available in one place."

I can almost feel the panic listening to Fabienne talk about her 3 am sweats! Let's learn more about how she turned things around.

Creating a client attraction system

"I went to this person over here for sales and I went to that person over there to learn more about networking and I had one book on how to position yourself in the marketplace and another about how to price your services so people buy them. Blood, sweat and tears later I figured out what worked for me, and what I noticed is that there were a lot of people saying a lot of great things but they weren't necessarily working for my business. I tried things and when they worked I would put them in an imaginary 'this works' box and everything else I left behind. I essentially created my own client-attraction system and I filled my practice to capacity. Eight months later I was paying off my debts and even had a waiting list. Other nutritionists were asking me how I'd achieved it, so I started sharing information with them, and little by little my client-attraction system developed.

"It only had five steps to start with, but when once the system had worked people would say, 'I've got a new client, tell me what else to do', so I shared more and more with them. The word spread, their friends who were chiropractors or acupuncturists or financial planners started asking me, 'Can I become a client of yours? I don't want to talk about nutrition; could you teach me to get clients?' For a while I had an unusual hybrid practice of teaching some people how to boil brown rice or how to make tofu taste great, and others about marketing and sales, closing the sale and using the internet. That's when I saw the door of opportunity.

"I stopped teaching the nutrition once I discovered that marketing was so much fun; it's fun when it works and once other people realise that. I have been teaching my client attraction system for ten years. It has grown massively and we now work with people all over the world, helping them get more clients, make more money and finally let them be able to do their purpose in the world. I've taken it further; I created products, workshops, mastermind groups, continuity programmes, membership sites and information products, because I realised that different people want to learn in different ways. Some people want to work one-to-one with me for a year, to grow their five-figure business to a six-figure one, or their six-figure business to the million-dollar mark. Others want to be part of a small group or they want to learn from an audio like an mp3, CD or tele-seminar or videos. That's the core of information marketing: showing people how to do something in whatever way they want to do it, If they are auditory people they buy the CDs, if they want to work with you directly, they hire you. That's how I started my own business. It's been an evolution."

Fabienne is in a great place, with her "yummy family life" and successful million-dollar virtual business, but how did she get started online? How did she change her strategy from seeing customers face-to-face to serving customers virtually?

Attracting more and more people

"A year or so into my business I started writing an email newsletter. I sent them to my clients, my friends and my family, and every time I added somebody new, they would send it on to somebody else, and so it would grow. Soon after, I started doing tele-classes which are training to a group by using a conference call service and inviting people to them whenever I went to a networking group. I would hand out flyers and then I started advertising them online and attracting people I didn't know. People signed up that didn't live in New York, they would be from, for example, San Francisco and I even had attendees from Europe. They would join my tele-classes and it worked well as, because I only had an hours-for-dollars business model-meaning people would see me face-to-face for an hourly fee, I actually transitioned my practice from in-person to on-the-phone, so I could work with people all around the world.

"It actually scared me that I was attracting so many people and my head was spinning because I didn't know how to handle all of the business that was coming, so believe it or not I stopped doing my newsletter completely for a year. But I realised that was crazy and I had to keep doing it. I started doing it in HTML so it was full colour, and started injecting some of my personality into it.

"At one point I had 32 clients at the same time and it was madness. I couldn't do everything myself; the administration, supplies, coaching, invoicing and taking the card payments. And I was still attracting more people, some of whom weren't in a position to pay my full fee, so I considered creating something that provided the same information but at a lower price point. It took me three years but I launched the client attraction home-study system, which is still our bestseller, as a downloadable product. It keeps selling because the information is so good and we're speaking to thousands and thousands of people every week. I then started doing group programmes. I did a ten-week boot-camp teaching the client attraction home-study system live; that was a leveraged way of dealing with 20 people per hour as opposed to one."

Making more money than my accountant

"I then reached a point where I was working with over 75 clients at the same time and I was suddenly making a lot more money. I remember going to see my accountant and when he saw what I was making his face went white. I had just arrived at his office, my daughter was a newborn, and here we were handing over our paperwork (and typically she decided to have a fit in his office). He could see I was a new mum, yet I was making more than he was. He didn't last very long as my accountant because I think he felt uncomfortable in that situation.

"From then on it went from my first workshop, my first mastermind group, my first continuity programme, my first workshop in a box, to where I could really focus on leveraging the business. In the first few years it was mostly one-to-one clients and I was selling the home-study system, so I was doing 93% hours-for-dollars and 7% passive-leveraged income. Now it's completely the opposite.

"The beautiful thing is that this business model allows you to be a mum. My number-one core value is my family and we've been able to create the income but I've been able to work from home the entire time. I tried to open an office in downtown New York at one stage because I thought to be a more serious business I needed that, but then I realised that I would be with my family much less. Having my office at home means I can spend time with my children before they go to school and have lunch with them.

"I have since had another baby and my husband has been able to walk away from his corporate job to help run my company. He's doubled his income and by using his expertise it allows us to all be together and that is what we wanted in the first place, this is why we do what we do. I help others because I will never forget what it was like not having enough money and clients; so now I am taking this message to as many people around the world as I can. I have a really great life and that's why this virtual business model is so great for mums."

I'm so inspired hearing about Fabienne's husband coming on board with the business and imagine how things might work out for me if my husband were to do the same! Fabienne explains how they have developed a programme to coach couples working together based on their experience.

Not killing each other

"We're actually doing a programme for people who are interested in working with their other half (www.workingwithyourspouse.com), it's still under the attracting-clients umbrella, but we're teaching other families how to do it. If you're in the position where unfortunately your husband has been laid-off or has chosen to leave his job, you can bring your husband onboard in your virtual business so he brings his skills to it. There needs to be systems in place for working together so you don't kill each other! It's not easy and there are a lot of communication issues to work on, a lot of administrative and operational issues and working on your strengths and weaknesses.

"I had to work on my mindset before opening up my own business. If I hadn't started doing personal growth and development and understanding the universal principles, whatever you want to call it, I don't know if I would have taken that great leap of faith to leave my corporate career all those years ago. It takes a lot of faith. If I were married at the time and I had a husband's income to support me it might have been easier, but I was walking away from a steady job and I was living in an apartment by myself in New York, which is one of the most expensive places to live. I had to have faith.

"Here's what I know now: having your own business is the fastest way to expand your mindset and

> 66 I help others because I will never forget what it was like not having enough money and clients. 99

" I had to have faith. " the best vehicle for personal growth and development because each time that you want to grow your business you must look within and clear out fears and limiting beliefs that do not serve you. What I mean is that there are a lot of people who are very content staying small because growing bigger in their business will mean that they will have to overcome their fear of being overwhelmed, fear of success, fear of what people will think of them. There's even a fear of alienating friends and family, which is what happened to me; my friends now are not the same friends I had when I was back in the corporate world, because when you go out and do something that is very big, it brings out people's inadequacies and you really have to dig deep and say, 'It's ok I'm going do it anyway'.

"There are many people who don't have the courage and they continue to live a mediocre life. I'm not being judgemental but they're living a dull colour life as opposed to living a life in full colour. Each time that you are presented an opportunity to go really big, like doing your very first workshop and marketing it all over the world, it really forces you to look within and have faith in yourself, and if you don't have faith in yourself then you have to work on all those beliefs and all those fears. "

The fastest path to personal development

"Having your own business and wanting it to be really big is the fastest path to personal development because you cannot grow without the right mindset. I'll give you an example, there may be hundreds of people who, before going through the client attraction process with me, are marketing until they're blue in the face. They're doing all the right things but not getting results, and that's because of all the things under the surface that they don't know are there. There are people who are wondering, 'Why am I doing all the right things but the income is not there?', but what you say you want for your business must absolutely match with what your subconscious beliefs are about it. Those two things must mirror your actions and your behaviours. For example, if somebody says, 'I want to make a million dollars' but then subconsciously thinks, 'I will be rejected' or 'Who do I think I am?', they don't believe that it could happen and they don't take the action, and without the action they don't get the results. So mindset is absolutely crucial.

" If you look at all the people who have made it really big in their businesses, you'll see they all have several things in common. The first is that they're excellent marketers. It's a skill that you're not born with, it is one you learn. Then you absolutely must have a mindset that is set on success, you must be mentored by someone who is already more successful than you and you should be part of a mastermind group with other high-achieving people. If you look around there is no one who has made it really big who doesn't have a mentor and colleagues that they mastermind with. There is rarely a self-made person. Usually there is a team behind that person and always a mentor showing them the way. "

Let's learn more about the team and mentor that have helped Fabienne along her way.

Distracted from making money

" If you want to grow your business you need a team in place. A team can start with just one part-time virtual assistant. I started with a virtual assistant many years ago and I could only afford to have her work with me ten hours a month. At the end of every week I would ask, 'How many hours are we at now?', but I only had her work on the things that were distracting me from making more money and once the money came, I increased her hours. I increased my

> ** You absolutely must have a mindset that is set on success. **

revenues dramatically because this person was able to take on the administrative side and that let me spend more time marketing my business. I worked with that person for five years before I brought in another person to do more of the basic administrative stuff and quickly brought on two more people and we just kept building.

" We currently have nine virtual assistants and we recently hired a full-time business manager so that they could take over a lot of my husband's things and he could start building his own branch of the business. I can hear someone thinking, 'Well that's fine for you because you have the income', but the only reason I have the income is because I have the team. In the very beginning it's often about bringing in someone part-time. I also got help on the personal side. We have an au pair for our two older children, a nanny for the third child and we have a housekeeper that comes in so that we can work on the business from home, knowing the children are close by and well cared for, leaving us real quality time with them.

" I'm sharing this because having all that support means that I can build the business and be stress-free; I don't have to worry about doing the laundry and buying birthday presents for children's parties, so when are we with the children we are really with them, and when we are with our business we are really with the business. A lot of mums working from home will understand the 'Hold on honey, just one more email and I'll be right with you' situation. Well, for me there's a lot less of that because we have the support. So it's not just about getting support in for the business, if you can hire someone for $10 an hour to run errands for you – even for just two hours a week – it makes a huge difference for the entrepreneurial mum. "

It's great that Fabienne is being so open about the domestic support she has, as well as the business support. Next, we explore why mums can feel guilty about getting help in and why we sometimes feel like we 'should' be able to do it all ourselves.

Cheating your business and cheating your children

" Guilt. We feel that when we're working we should be with the children, but we're not fully with them if we're trying to work while making dinner or playing with them. You're also cheating your business if you try to work while your children are around, so you might as well separate them and then when you're with your children you can really be in the moment and when you're with your business you're super focused.

" You can do a lot more in a lot less time because you don't have distractions and interruptions, and you're honouring those separate parts of your life. You can be a whole woman that way as opposed to being a mother who doesn't give 100% to any part of her life. The very sophisticated system that we have at home is that on mummy's office door, there's a big smiley face that says 'mummy's free' and on the other side there's a sad face saying 'mummy's busy' (my six-year-old can read the sign and my son who's only four can see the sad face and knows not to knock on the door). When mummy's not busy, the door is open, or there's the happy face or mummy is downstairs. Believe it or not something as simple as that works wonders.

" These are all the things that nobody talks about but they're absolutely crucial for us mumpreneurs because it's going to be extremely difficult to have the kind of business that brings in lots of money and that means lots of freedom, so these things must be handled. I don't want people to think that I'm this overly strict, always 'by-the-book' kind of person. In fact, I'm quite the opposite. I'm more of a loosey-goosey, fun 'Oh well, we didn't take a bath today, so we'll take one tomorrow' kind of person. It doesn't have to be that way, but in having systems, I've found that I've created so much freedom because most things are taken care of and that leaves me a lot of time for my kids. I think it's really important. I hear women trying to do it all, but what I see is they're depressed, they're usually drinking too much wine at night or they're just unrealistic. What

I from my days in nutrition counselling is that unexpressed emotions can become toxic in the body. If you have all this unexpressed resentment then that can manifest later on into something that's unhealthy for you. Take care of yourself along the way."

Having more energy makes you more attractive

"I wouldn't be able to have the kind of business and the kind of income that I have if I didn't have all this support. I also take a no-excuses approach to ending the day at 5.30 pm It didn't use to be that way. When I was single, sometimes I worked until 8.00 pm or 10.00 pm or sometimes even 1.00 am because I enjoyed it so much. Now, the minute the kids come home from school, the play date or whatever, all the computers in the house get shut down. We all go downstairs, play together and start our evening as a family.

"Sometimes I'll do a tele-class in the evening, but really you have to take a no-excuses approach about ending the day. If you just keep going and going, when do you replenish yourself? You're just going to drive yourself into the ground. A tired woman is not good for her family and is not client attractive. The more energy you have, the more clients you can attract, and the more money you can make. The more money you can make, the more conveniences you can have in your life, and the more people you can hire on your team."

Parents need energy, it's just the way it is, so what are we going to do to make sure that we have the energy to give our children attention, to really listen and talk to them, to read with them, to teach them basic skills, to play and to have the patience of a saint with them? The MMs certainly give a lot of energy to their businesses so why does it seem to work so well compared to giving energy to a job. Maybe it's not having to commute, maybe it's not having to put up with the office politics or the lack of control over your role, maybe it's not having the threat of redundancy or pay cuts?

I'm not minimising the stress that a business can bring too, especially in the start-up phase, but at least in your own business you can outsource support when you are overwhelmed and are free to make all the decisions as Fabienne has done. I'm intrigued and thrilled that Fabienne's business has contributed so much to the wealth of the family that her husband Derek has quit his corporate career to come on board and will be doubling his income. After all, isn't it usually the other way round?

MEET SHERI MCCONNELL

"SMART WOMEN CREATE
MEMBERSHIP-BASED
BUSINESSES"

Sheri McConnell is a smart woman. She has grown her virtual business past a million dollars and went into multi-million figures in 2010, all while working from home as a mum of four and before the age of 40. Sheri is the CEO of Sheri McConnell Companies Inc., www.sherimcconnell.com, and is also the president of two associations, the Smart Women's Institute of Entrepreneurial Learning, www.smartwomeninstitute.com, and the Global Institute of Associations, www.gia-connect.com. She's also the author of *Smart Women Create Membership-Based Businesses* and *The Smart Women's Book of Powerful Quotations.*

Sheri's motivation comes from empowering women to achieve financial independence by learning how to leverage their time, money, and expertise exponentially. She believes that when a woman is financially independent, she makes decisions from a healthier place on behalf of herself and her family, and when you teach a woman how to achieve financial independence you empower many generations to come. Sheri is known as a leader to leaders and consults with big thinkers and creators from all over the world in multiple industries, teaching them how to leverage the association-business model. Sheri says:

> *I enjoy a lot of freedom in my life. Freedom to spend more time with my four kids, freedom to stay in shape, and freedom to earn more than I ever did in the corporate world and way more than I ever dreamed I could owning my own businesses. Today I am able to work from my home office in San Antonio, Texas. And the best part is I am able to work with my ideal customers on a daily basis – many of them six and seven-figure earners themselves.*

But it hasn't always been like this. Sheri has struggled and persevered to build the virtual business she enjoys today. So when did Sheri decide to go into business and what was happening in her life at the time?

SHERI'S STORY

"I left the corporate world when I had my third child. Day care for one child runs close to a thousand dollars and I already had two children under the age of three, so when I had my third child it simply wasn't worth it, even with a very successful corporate job. And that's when I decided to stay at home. While staying at home raising my children I wanted to find something to do with *all* that extra time that I was going to have now! I just knew I had to do something that plugged in to my passion.

"If you've had urges or an inkling of being an entrepreneur it's something that's in you and I believe it's largely innate. You might not ever act on it, but you have probably always wanted to do something very independent. That was me and when I was at home after my third child, sitting breastfeeding for the whole year, I decided to dig back into my passion."

Having this time away from the rat race and the time to think really helped Sheri to explore the idea of starting a business.

"Because I had the opportunity to be at home with the kids, taking a break from the routine of working and taking kids back and forth to day care and not even having time to read a book, I felt so grateful to be at home. My husband was paying the bills and was actually home for 12 weeks and gone for 12 weeks so I raised them by myself half the time."

Sheri certainly made good use of the time she spent breastfeeding that year because after months of reading and research she had come up with a business idea that tapped into her passion for writing. What's interesting, though, is that Sheri understood how hard it was to make money from writing and realised that serving the writing industry would be more rewarding, planting the seed for her first business. Sheri shares the story of that very first aha! moment.

Finding an easier way

"I've dug into something that I previously loved and that was writing, so my advice is whatever you do, even if you don't know the path in front of you yet, if you have an opportunity to explore a business that you think you might love to do, it starts with your passion. I started reading all the books about writing, I subscribed to *Writer's Digest* magazine at first, and when I opened it there were endless amounts of books and referrals for businesses, books and websites, so I just started there. By the end of that first year of breastfeeding, with a book in one hand and the other hand on my baby's cute little head, I really understood the industry. I knew who the players were, great ways to make money and what to avoid in that particular industry, so one thing I love to tell people – especially mums – is to honour your faith. Wherever you're at, even if doesn't feel like you're working, you are working.

"I wasn't particularly working on my business that year but I was moving forward because when I was able to put fingers to a keyboard and really put some hours in, I had a lot of knowledge about the industry and that really helped me get started. I started on the internet because the first thing I knew just from reading all those books was that I didn't want to be a writer. I wanted to be the one serving the writing industry because I didn't want to make money the way they were. It was just too hard. As the industry is so big I saw potential to serve the people within it, and that's when I came up with the idea for the association model – having paid memberships to a professional association. That was my first aha! moment. I decided to serve them instead of being one of them."

Getting it off the ground

"Between 2001 and 2006 I focused on growing that one particular association. The internet gave me the ability to find experts and leverage the association business model. There's a lot about this model that makes it so attractive and that's why I was able to move so fast. I was able to leverage all the ways that people view the association model, how they treat it, the respect that they gave me and just kept moving forward. The internet had started to become much more efficient and the cost of technology was decreasing.

"After interviewing so many successful (multi-millionaire) entrepreneurs for the National Association of Women Writers (NAWW) one thing we found was that all serial entrepreneurs get one business off the ground before they go on to the next one. One of the most common mistakes is that a person often gets frustrated because their business is not taking off and he/she moves too quickly to the next business. It really does require focusing in on that one business, going back to the drawing board and reinventing that business so that it gets to the transformational point. When you're plugging into a coaching programme or a mastermind group, you're bypassing that struggle of trying to figure everything out yourself. That's what you're paying for in a coaching programme; you're leveraging your money instead of your time to shortcut the process."

If only she'd had a coach then! So when did Sheri start to see the transformation in her business?

Hitting the wall

"Around year two or three I experienced some big breakthroughs simply by starting to say no. Success is more about what you say no to than what you say yes to, and most people say yes to everything for the first few years. They burn themselves out, they get near quitting and finally they have to hit this really hard brick wall. It's only then they decide to do it a different way; their way. For some reason everybody seems to have to get to that point before they're willing to do it the way they should have done it from the beginning. If you have someone who can tell you what some of those mistakes look like then you can do it a lot faster (and you can skip the painful wall-hitting step!).

" It's a typical scenario because most people get blocked. Women, especially, get blocked around cash flow, for example they're too nervous to go and get that loan so that they can shortcut the process. What they're really saying deep down is that they don't believe in their own abilities and they're not willing to take the risk, and to be fair a lot of that is because everything in their external environment is screaming the same thing. My passion and our mission at my company is to help women leverage their knowledge and reach financial independence. "

My wall

" The turning point for me was hitting that brick wall, looking at NAWW and saying to myself, 'Right, I'm going to do it this way. I'm going to charge what I know it's worth. Even if just a quarter of the members remain it's going to be exactly the same return as what I'm getting now'. I knew we were worth it and that's the brick wall I had to hit, and it completely changed the company for me.

" Being so inexperienced, when I started I cut myself some slack. But when I started to peel back the layers of the other international association for women writers that existed at that time I could see that they were struggling too. I had gone and copied a struggling company, but once I started figuring those things out that's when I started to be a leader. I think it's really common that in the first few years you follow. You're not confident enough to lead on your own unless you invest in some coaching to help you become that leader. One of things that I'm doing in my business now is turning leaders into visionaries. I'm really helping to change who they are and it's all about mindset."

Note to self; don't model your business on a struggling one. So where was Sheri getting her inspiration from once she realised the company she was modelling wasn't exactly the best example?

Learning the entrepreneurial world

"The beautiful thing about having an association is you have a place to invite amazingly brilliant people. I have been lucky enough to interview so many people and bring that knowledge to my members. Plus I have made lots of really great solid business relationships. It meant that I was learning at the same time my members were learning.

"One of the great things about the association model is you're always moving forward as you're serving your people. Now I work with amazing people who aren't in the writing industry and consult with many different industries. In the last ten years I've been lucky enough to have companies in multiple industries and through my coaching I get to learn about industries I would never get to experience, like neuroscience. I'm there to teach them the association model. I know nothing about neuroscience but I get to learn all about the industry. I get to work with people who are starting associations for different industries. Don't be afraid to cross into other industries and take things that are working well in other industries and bring it back to your own."

So when did the business begin it's transformation to virtual?

Leverage

"A big shift in the company was moving from the NAWW chapters and physical locations for meetings, to going completely virtual. That served my purpose and it served who I wanted to be and the type of company I wanted to run. I wanted to go global, be more virtual and progress faster. Running all the chapters and having physical annual conferences took so much time, energy and money that it limited the company to a certain size and meant I was spending less time with my family. It was a conscious shift and I was very happy to do it.

"There are three things that every business has to leverage: time, money and expertise. I love to leverage other people's conferences. I gather leads, or give away free books at booths. I have staff there helping me out and I'm consciously leveraging someone else's conference. I've learned from doing conferences the hard way. I did four of them at the NAWW and then took a lot of time off! Conferences are seriously big budget in both time and money and we now need a strategic reason why we do or don't do them.

"I also leverage my knowledge into information products. I love teaching mums about them, because it takes their knowledge and puts it in a form that people can buy over and over again. You can literally create a six-figure business with a good information product that's $297. I teach people how to do it all the time."

Sheri has been so open about how her thinking held her back at first; let's explore how her mindset has changed as she has grown her business.

Positive energy

"A business needs support, cash flow and positivity. It needs positive energy, and that's one of the things that I didn't understand.

"Early on I couldn't leverage cash flow so what I leveraged was my time. I thought, if I could do it with three kids under my feet at home, anybody can! So sometimes I was copying brochures with a child crawling around my feet. I still got those brochures copied but I remember thinking, 'Why am I doing this?' It was all part of my personal journey because I didn't have the cash flow and was stuck in my mindset. I went really slowly at the beginning, and did all of the things I tell people not to do now! Once I started figuring these things out I made great progress."

Learning about the entrepreneurial world and being part of that world must have involved risk for Sheri as the very essence of being an entrepreneur is about taking measured risks for reward. What's Sheri's take on risk?

Walking through the fear

"These days I feel really good about taking risks and implementing what I've learned over the years. Many of our core growth strategies are the same as we were using back then: an online newsletter to build a list and gathering leads for different products and services. Some of the core foundations are still exactly the same and some of the mistakes that people make are exactly the same! There's a lot of information out there so it's get clear about what you say yes to and what you say no to. An easy way to do that is to think, 'If it's not a hell yes it's a hell no!' If you have an opportunity but you're not sure and you're only saying yes because you think that it might pay the bills, then sometimes that leaves you back in a place that you don't want to be in – we've all been there.

"I've always focused on the one area that I wanted to grow, for example, when I wanted to get my own book published or when I wanted to engage in public speaking. I actually created the accountability within my own company to make those things happen. For the first few conferences I was doing all I could; I remember waking up in the middle of the night six months beforehand and being completely freaked out about being in front of all those women. And I wasn't even speaking; I was just the MC! That's nerve-wrecking bad public speaking used to be for me. Then I read a great book about breathing techniques (I actually still have it on my shelf today) and discovered that I was actually hyperventilating. I never realised that before. Had I not created that conference and found that book I would have never got over that fear.

"Over the years I've grown by feeling the fear and walking straight through it. I had moments of 'Why am I doing this?', but I knew why – because I wanted to get to that other end. I wanted to get past it. I wanted to grow, and once you do that once or twice you get it. For every goal after that you walk through the fear much more easily, but those first few times are the ones where you just don't know if you'll survive! It gets easier after the first few, you get the reward and from then on it's a case of, 'I feel the fear, but I'm moving forward anyway'.

"The risks don't stop whatever level you're at but the opportunities keep coming, so you have to sit there and look at your return on investment with everything that comes at you. There's always something new. As with most things, the first time you do it, it's really hard and then you get better at it."

It's really interesting to learn that risk never goes away in business; that's if you want to continue growing. Bigger and better opportunities will come up and you have to get comfortable with accepting risk.

Be that leader

"You're putting yourself out there. It's like that for a lot of people and this is why I'm really good at tough love when I'm coaching. Once people have a few sessions with me I can get straight to the source because I can see behaviours – I've done just about every one of them! I can zero right in on it. I've got really great results and I love people writing to me saying that I'm helping. That's the whole point isn't it?

"When there's just too much going on – trust me, I have four kids, my youngest is three, I understand – you need a coach and I need a coach too. In the early years I was propping up other people. I have a bachelors' degree in social work and that's what I always did. For the longest time I wouldn't get out there and be the expert, so I had to be pushed to do that. I had all kinds of reasons why I wasn't willing to, yet I wanted it. My coaches have really helped me and that's what I now do for other people. I really push them to be leaders because I know that's where they can create the most positive change. The fastest and quickest way to create change is to be a leader."

Sheri recommends Seth Godin's book, *Tribes*, as a great resource to learn more about why the world needs leaders and suggests that everyone today has an opportunity to start a movement. Seth says:

> *Too many people ignore the opportunity to lead because they are 'sheepwalking' their way through their lives and work, too afraid to question whether their compliance is doing them, or their company, any good. If you have a passion for what you do and the drive to make it happen, there is a tribe of fellow employees, or customers, or investors or readers just waiting for you to connect them with each other and lead them where they want to go.*

I loved Seth's book too. It supports much of what I have created in my Supermummy business and Sheri's association model.

"Read Seth's book, then read my membership-based business model book and you'll want to start an association. Seth's book is in line with what I've been saying for years, but he says it in a different way; he never uses the word 'associations', he calls it 'tribes', you're building your tribes. It's very powerful and this is the way business is going. Traditional business is changing completely to keep up with the internet."

So how does a leader and visionary like Sheri have time for her business, her family and her self? Sheri reveals all.

Act like a CEO

"A huge piece of how you can do this and still have balance and sanity is to put support systems in place. My team is half virtual and half local. I have three ladies that live locally and come into my home office. I also have some team members down the street but they work virtually. The first job I recommend outsourcing is your website; I don't like anyone to build their own site. It never works out and it doesn't do the job it needs to. The second job, and this is what so many people don't do, is to outsource someone for your customer service. Think like a CEO and act like a CEO as quickly as you can. Remove yourself from the front lines and don't answer the generic emails and phone calls yourself.

"Even if you start by only hiring someone for a couple of hours a month or a couple of hours a week at $40 an hour, that $80 dollars will catapult you forward because you won't be handling so much of the basic admin that gets in the way and slows you down. Customer services can sometimes be people arguing with you. It often happens at the beginning because people tend to do that when they know you're new. If you can only afford two hours per month then that's where you start. That will move you forward much faster and you can work on your mindset because you've removed all the admin that keeps road blocking you. The biggest advantage for me, being a mother of four, in having a great team, is when I have sick kids."

We can all relate to that. It's such a huge dilemma for a working mum about what to do when you have a sick child at home. Being the boss of your own company and having a team in place will keep things running if you ever need time out to care for your kids, or yourself. We get sick too. What would happen if you were really ill and forced to take time out, time away, from your business? This actually happened to Sheri; she caught pneumonia and needed to take complete bed rest. Unless you saw some of her Facebook or Twitter updates you probably would have had no idea, because while she was resting her business was running like clockwork.

Sheri goes on to explain how she has had to overcome some personal issues around getting help. Like Fabienne and Alexis, Sheri is responsible for a million-dollar business and it's moving into the multi-millions so it's hardly surprising that she needs support for both her business and her family. While she still works from her home office – keeping her close to her family and allowing her to be strict about logging off when the kids come home – the fact is she has a business to run. It's refreshing to hear that she had the usual 'mother's-guilt syndrome' when accepting help, and knowing that support is helping her to achieve her mission is important.

66 Traditional business is changing completely to keep up with the internet. 99

Helping women become financially independent

"To be completely honest it took a lot of years for me and my husband to really share the workload, and it was proportional to how the income grew. I find that's also true with the people that I coach. Now when I travel I really rely on my team to help me with my kids, and that was a huge shift as a mother. I've had to change and evolve.

"Some of my personal struggles and issues along the way were about my life looking so different than everybody else's, but I've got used to that now and my family is happy. People even help me buy my groceries when I'm short of time. I have all these great mums around me. That's why I have locals on my team, because I employ them, they help me and I love it because it's in line with the mission of the company, which is helping women become financially independent.

"There are a lot of things I've learned about building a team. I made the mistake of hiring entrepreneurs; typically if you hire an entrepreneur they need to go off and start their own business, they don't want to be an employee. At a certain point you need more employees that don't ever want to be entrepreneurs. That's a hiring technique that I teach; I teach a lot of team stuff because that's a big part to getting past the six figures."

Honour your faith

"We'll be going into multi-millions this year. We have a whole new set of mastermind programmes. I'm very excited about it. I love this part. One of the things I've been doing strategically is within the next few years I want to have ten 'Smart Women' books available. We'll build on the brand and will be funnelling leads into our 'Smart Women' success programme. Over the years I've invested in myself and my companies by hiring mentors to help me progress faster. I invested six figures in my own mentor but what it did to my business was huge. There's so much accountability for doing that, but also a whole different way of people seeing me and the positioning it had on my business.

"The belief I have in myself and what I could launch next year is huge. It's amazing what a mum at home with a lot of kids can do! Over the years it took me believing in myself more than anybody else, not my family, not my husband, not my kids. Nobody believed in me. I had to do that for myself. I had to be the person that made it happen. I always tell people to honour their faith. If you're having a down day and feel like you hate your business, that's okay, take time off from it and when the passion comes back you come back to it."

Sheri is now commanding fees of $100,000 for her own one-year private-coaching programme. Can you imagine writing a cheque for that? What if you knew you could be getting a ten-fold return on that investment; would you feel happier about getting your cheque book out then? It's the same principle as spending $100 on some coaching to make $1000 from your business, it's just the amount that changes.

Investing in business or personal coaching can be a wise decision. Sheri attributes huge growth in her business to high-quality coaching and she also helps others get results through her coaching programmes. Coaching by itself is no guarantee of success, you still have to do the work and follow through on plans to see results, but as there is so much free advice out there paying a coach to make sure you don't settle for less could be a good investment.

Sheri had already built a solid foundation for her business and was successful in many ways, but her decision to invest in a high-end coaching programme seems to have been the catalyst for a big expansion. Could she have done it without the coaching? Who knows, but what I do know is that Sheri's passion is undeniable and she truly is a leader and visionary and, having met her, she is warm, calm and considerate too. A Smart Woman and a Supermummy!

CHANGE THE WAY YOU WORK AND LIVE

So there's the proof. It's possible to make a million working from home and actually be happier and more fulfilled. Even if a million seems too far out of reach then just to be able to replace your current income with money made from your own home business would be a fantastic start. I believe that by following the examples of women like these MMs, working mums have the opportunity to re-invent themselves because women today have more choices than ever concerning career and family matters and now we have the option of starting a business from home using the internet as a tool to grow our businesses.

In these stories you saw some of the same basic steps repeated and similar strategies employed, and even though the MMs have different businesses their basic structures are the same. They have all leveraged what they know, taken advantage of technology to scale their businesses and have avoided needing employees on the payroll by using automated systems and outsourcing support. They have found a way to be unique in how they execute their business, and of course as individuals, but look closely and you'll see nothing new about their core business. This is great news for you, as coming up with 'the big idea' can be a real stumbling block to getting started. You don't necessarily have to go through the process of inventing and patenting a product to sell to make serious money.

Now you know you can make money from what you know. If you're still having a mental block about what you can sell through your virtual business it may be that you are taking for granted the skills, knowledge and expertise that you have developed. You simply need information that others want and are willing to pay for, that can be delivered in a variety of ways when it's convenient to them.

Are you ready to challenge the status quo? To escape the drudgery and do something you are passionate about? To make money immersed in work that stimulates and fulfills you? To secure a future of exciting opportunities? What might it be costing you emotionally to not take action? What might the benefits of doing this be in, say, ten years' time? What do you really have to lose from at least testing a business?

You don't need permission to start a website, to start researching your idea, to start building relationships with people who are interested in what you do and say, so why not go for it? Not ready yet? You'll never be truly ready for change, which is inevitable, so the question is whether you want to proactively create this change or whether you will continue to follow the majority and react to changes that will undoubtedly be forced upon you. Read on to learn more about how the MMs have changed the way they work and live and how you can too.

INTRODUCING THE MOST FLEXIBLE BUSINESS MODEL EVER

A virtual business

There are many commonalities in the millionaire mumpreneur stories and I'll cover them all in detail in the next chapter. What stands out is that they are all running virtual businesses. They are ordinary women, from different backgrounds, different countries, different walks of life and with different interests who have created extraordinary lifestyles, wealth and positive influences on others from scratch, and in some cases very quickly and with limited resources. Some had business experience before going virtual. Others did not. There is nothing inherently 'special' about them that is lacking in you. Their stories reveal more about their mindset than their qualifications. They may serve different markets, have different products and offer different services but the structure of their businesses is the same: virtual.

Information nation

I gave you a brief overview of what makes a virtual business at the start of the book and how it differs from the 'traditional' approach. What helps to make these businesses totally virtual is that they are all marketing information. What are most people doing while they are online? Searching for information. In our 'now' society it's getting easier and easier to access information and there is an increasing demand for quality content. If you can identify a market with a high interest in specific information and then provide it in a varied and convenient way then you've got yourself a business.

Marketing information encompasses products such as books, manuals, home-study courses, DVDs, CDs, audio services, video services, eBooks, tele-coaching, group coaching, membership programmes, seminars and conferences. What makes a virtual business so flexible is the ability to take what you know, create a product or service providing that information, and then sell it over and over again to clients all over the world. You can start with one product or service, giving you your first income stream, and then add more as you grow, and because the margins are so good it's more about what the information is worth than what the materials or technology actually cost.

Work from anywhere

Your website is the location of your business and all the support you need to run your business can be outsourced, e.g. by having a virtual assistant. So now you can not only work from home but from anywhere with internet access, and by taking advantage of many of the automated solutions available you don't necessarily have to be sat at your computer for eight hours a day. Get technology and other people to work for you while you work smart on the productive tasks that will grow your business.

To face or not to face?

You can choose to continue seeing clients on a one-to-one basis or at live events or have no personal interaction with them. Either way it's still possible for a virtual business to give a personal touch. These MMs still interact with their customers but even that can be made virtual through tele-seminars, webinars and coaching programmes. You could make a million without ever meeting a single one of your customers face-to-face, but the reality is that to get started you may need to adopt the one-to-one approach and then transition to virtual products and services once you have started generating income and have some experience with real-life clients. Ultimately, you make the rules with a virtual business model so if there is a demand from your customers or a need in you to serve people face-to-face or by doing a live event then do so, but it's also possible to remain totally virtual and make a difference; find the way that best suits you.

The way forward

This way of doing business is perfect for a mum who needs flexibility and yet is still not represented that well in the UK. Until now! If you do a general search for work-from-home opportunities you'll come across a variety of options such as commission only cold calling and buying into a franchise. When it comes to ideas for making money from an online business many mums will be familiar with the concept of advertising revenue from a website and selling goods online but they may not have considered building an online business based on what they know, either from their current career skills or from a creative talent or passion. What do you know that you could coach others in? What experience do you have that could be really helpful to others?

We're virtually there

To recap, selling information works when you have a target market with a high interest in a topic or area and you then package information into products and services to match that interest and sell them online. This entire process, including taking the orders and the delivery of products and services, can be completely virtual. There are few businesses that allow you to duplicate yourself in this way; you create a product once and then sell it over and over again, serving many clients at the same time.

Although success isn't necessarily easy, after studying many information marketers and the MMs it's clear that success comes from doing things in a certain way. So there is a process, but first here's a reminder of the various products and services offered by the MMs, some virtual, some in person:

- Ezines – Emailed newsletter for generating leads and building a relationship

- eBooks – pdf download with cover design

- Audios – mp3 download or CD

- Manuals – pdf download

- Tele-seminars – Group seminars conducted over the phone

- Webinars – Online tutorials using a combination of video, sharing slides and screen sharing

- Videos – Online streaming videos (think YouTube!)

- Books – Published books (old school, but still popular)

- Membership website – Password-only access to paying members

- Group coaching programme – Any combination of the above supplied to lots of people

- Mastermind or retreat – A live group event

- Information products – A home-study system potentially containing a combination of printed manuals, checklists, questionnaires, instructions, audio CD, and videos/DVD

- Seminars or conferences – Public speaking to promote you and your business

Get supported

Let's face it, at the beginning you'll probably be on a shoestring budget and will be doing most of the work, if not all of it, yourself. This isn't necessarily a bad thing because it's your business and you need to know it inside and out so you can update the people you are outsourcing to, whether that's a bookkeeper, admin or virtual assistant. If your first virtual product is getting ten orders per week or you have ten people in your first coaching programme then you can handle everything yourself. You can manually take orders over the phone, deal with customer enquiries and answer every email personally. But what happens when you have 100 orders or clients, or 1000? With this virtual business model if you can sell to one client you can sell to 1000, it simply comes down to the marketing, so looking after 1000 paying clients is possible.

As the number of orders increases so will your time spent on customer service and now the time you are spending answering calls and emails and sending orders is taking you away from time spent on new business growth, hence it's important to get help. Okay, so someone else may not do something in exactly the way that you would, but at least it's done. You can only make money from things that are done so go for good, accurate productivity over perfectionism. Add an FAQ section to your website to show the people you are outsourcing your administration and how you want your company to be represented. You might want to issue standard procedures and scripts to guide them, and perhaps give them authority to make specific customer-services-related decisions, such as dealing with refund requests. Make it simple for them to do their job without having to check every minor detail with you first. You'll only make huge leaps with a virtual business by letting go of any compulsion to make everything perfect and getting out of your team's way so that you are not being the bottleneck.

So what do you do?

Building a virtual business might make it more difficult to answer the question 'So what do you do?'; watch the puzzled look on their face as you explain this mysterious lifestyle you lead. How could you possibly explain to someone at the school gates how you make money from home and expect them to understand if they aren't familiar with this virtual business model? That you make more in a month working a few days a week from home than you used to earn in a whole year when you had a 'proper' job! People don't usually want to be millionaires just for the sake of saying it. A million in the bank isn't the dream. The dream is the freedom and lifestyle you believe that it will bring you. So the goal here is to free up more of your time and automate your income. To have others work for you rather than working for yourself. It's a simple mindset shift from being your own boss to being a business owner and taking your role seriously. If you simply want a small business that doesn't quite make enough to get you past the tax threshold, that's okay, but if the idea of creating wealth from a business without some of the 'trappings' of the 'traditional' way of doing business intrigues you then I hope you don't allow doubt and fear to stop you.

How do you feel now?

You now know that it's possible to make a million while working from home and raising a young family. How does the thought of doing that make you feel? Excited, motivated, inspired or terrified of the uncertainty of going it alone? Think about it this way; if this idea excites you but also makes you feel scared then what's the absolute worst-case scenario? What would it take to recover if it didn't work out? What is the risk anyway? What we fear doing most is usually what we most need to do. What might you be putting off out of fear? What's so scary about starting a blog, website or ezine anyway? Remember Karen started out with a blog, ezine and an eBook so you have nothing to fear. Life's too short!

Where to start

Putting fears aside, let's say you have a skill that people could or do pay you for. It may be your current job or previous career skills or something you do as a hobby or a passion. Now let's assume that instead of being employed by someone else to do this skill you decide you want to work for yourself.

One of the simplest ways to get started in business is to serve clients on a one-to-one basis. This could also be your entry into starting a virtual business because after you have gained experience and confidence you can then start to introduce some virtual services and then move on to creating more in-depth information products. You can still start with a website and build a database of prospective clients in return for something like an email newsletter while you get paid for seeing clients in person and become more familiar with the products that might be the most effective for you. Here's an illustration of what this process might look like:

One-to-one Clients	Leveraging Yourself Online	Information Products
Paid by the hour or by the job while building a database through your website	Serving many clients with virtual services, e.g. teleseminar, webinar, eBooks and coaching programmes	Packaging information into multi-media, e.g. home study courses, manual, DVDs and CDs

SUCCESS

"SUCCESS LEAVES CLUES"

The best way to inspire someone is to do it yourself and make them feel like they can do it too. Now that you have read stories of successful MMs you know that it can be done. You *can* do it too. You just need to know how. You need the strategy. Even if you achieve a fraction of their results you could still make a good income, do what you enjoy, work from home and be around more for your kids. In our society starting a business is often perceived as risky, reckless and unrealistic. I believe that this attitude is changing and with the risk of redundancy maybe being an employee isn't necessarily the most secure option! So long as you keep the risks low and don't put yourself in jeopardy, starting out in business might just be one of the best things you've ever done. The more mums that become successful in business, the easier it will be for others to follow, and maybe we can lead from the bottom by designing our working lives around our family instead of the other way around.

Modelling

Within these stories I have searched for the common basic steps, the same strategies implemented and the structure of their businesses to create a model for you to learn and copy, because in order for you to get from where you are now to where you want to be you need a proven plan. Knowing what to do simply isn't enough to guarantee success, though. You need a mentor or coach who won't allow you to settle for less, a peer group who will raise your standards and self-expectations, and then you need to consistently take action and measure your progress against your desired outcome. If you find you are not progressing then that's when a mentor, coach and peer group can really help you to unlock what's stopping you and power through it.

I've already introduced you to modelling, which is the most natural form of learning. Watch any child and see how they learn what to do and say from copying others. Of course, it's just as easy to model negative behaviour as it is positive! As adults we often forget that this powerful learning tool is there to help us learn and grow. The quickest path to success in anything is to model yourself on someone who is achieving the kind of life or accomplishing things that appeal to you. More often than not they have been through the struggle to get where they are and you can shortcut the process simply by studying their effective strategies and applying them to your life. Don't do it the hard way, take the path of mastery, but to master something you've got to be a student first.

Study this business model based on the experience of the mumpreneurs in this book and ask yourself: 'How can I apply this in my life? What steps can I take now?'

Recipe for Success

- **Success Assessment** – Can your idea realistically be run as a virtual business? What skills, knowledge, talent or creativity could you build an information-based business on? Is there a demand for that kind of information? Could you make the transition from delivering your service in person to going virtual?

- **Success Planning** – Do you now where you want to go? What is your vision? How can you simultaneously have cash flow now and make plans for scaling the business? How can you measure and celebrate your progress? What does success look like to you? How can you scale your business up from one-to-one clients to serving many clients at the same time? What are the milestones?

- **Success Mindset** – What kind of energy are you putting out? How can you attract customers? Are you open to opportunities? What are your beliefs about wealth? What is your relationship like with money? How much do you want to make? What are you passionate about?

- **Successful Collaboration** – Could you leverage both your expertise and that of others? What relationships can you build on? Is there a community of like-minded people you can join? Where can you do some quality networking? Who could you join forces with? What contacts have you already got that could support you?

- **Successful Investing - in yourself** – How can you continue to educate yourself? Where can you find a good mentor? What kind of coaching do you need? What events could you attend to keep up-to-date and motivated?

- **Risking Success** – How could you test your business idea? What's your intuition telling you? Are you planning to experiment with different strategies to grow your business? Will you consistently push yourself out of your comfort zone? What will you do when you're overcome with doubt and fear?

- **Successful Virtual Team** – Who might you need to support you? How can you prevent getting overwhelmed and burnout? What tasks are you always putting off? What can be done quicker, better or cheaper by outsourcing it to someone else?

The next section is a detailed analysis to help you understand each step of the business model. A combination of all these steps is required to get the best results, meaning if you took one away the model would not be as powerful. For example, if you had everything in place but your mindset was not congruent you would be sabotaging your success, or if you were ready for success with the right mindset but you didn't have a plan in place you may also be hindering your chances of success.

❝ To get from where you are now to where you want to be you need a proven plan. ❞

SUCCESS ASSESSMENT

You need to be brutally honest with yourself right from the start about whether your business idea can realistically get you the results you want and what you may need to do to turn it into a virtual business. For example, if you were planning to sell goods online, particularly something that you design and manufacture, that may not necessarily be a business that you can make totally virtual. If you are required to make something to fulfil an order then you may end up trapped by doing the work, and if you do get a surge in orders how will you have enough time to run your business and make your product? Even if you don't make the product yourself, you still need to deal with missing orders or shipments, payment difficulties, etc. Depending on the mark-up price of your products you may also find that you need to sell a huge amount to be in a position to pay yourself, so distribution is going to be a major factor. Selling goods through a website may work to prove that what you design or create sells but I would suggest that you're only likely get a real breakthrough by getting your product sold through the more influential retailers.

In that type of business you can only make one product and serve one customer at a time. The same applies if you are in a job or already have a business where you see customers face-to-face. You can only see one person an hour and only have so many available hours in the day. Transforming to virtual means you can either cut down on some of the one-to-one work by creating more virtual income streams, or go completely virtual and make your service available to anyone in the world because you no longer need to see people in person. You might decide that hiring a coach or mentor with this expertise right from the start will help you to clarify how you can either adapt your business or structure a virtual business from your idea. Most of the MMs in this book didn't start out with a completely virtual business, instead they implemented more and more virtual products and services over time.

Fabienne made a complete turnaround from 93% of her time spent individually with local customers to 93% of her time now spent serving thousands of people all over the world through her products and programmes.

There's no reason why you can't start out this way and take the fast route to virtual. Assess your business. Think about how you can leverage your knowledge and serve people virtually. Explore what work you will actually do yourself and what work others can do for you. Discover ways in which your business can be open 24/7 and yet you can arrange your own schedule. Remember, this model is not about working one-to-one with customers or creating a product to sell to one person at a time, so make a realistic assessment of how you can apply the virtual model to your business.

> **Think about how you can leverage your knowledge and serve people virtually.**

SUCCESS PLANNING

Starting an online business doesn't mean that you don't need a business plan and an internet business doesn't guarantee success so business principals still apply. Even if you are funding your start-up costs without the need to borrow any money, you still need a short, medium and long-term plan for your business. If you don't know where you are going, how will you know how far you've come and when you get there? The benefit of an online business, though, is that you don't necessarily need a detailed business plan because you can largely test your business by getting it in front of potential paying customers. You have the opportunity to get instant feedback on your ideas, which gives you the great advantage of being able to improve or adapt things as you go. In other words you can 'road test' your business before you put your heart, soul and savings into it!

There are certain things from the cornucopia of knowledge now available that are genuinely useful and apply to everyone, such as finding your target market. Then there are other things where there are no hard-and-fast rules, for example, how you set up your site, your blog and your social networking. Allow yourself the confidence and freedom to find your voice. You can define how you're going to do things. I really encourage you to find the way that works for you but whatever you do, have a plan.

A business plan is fundamental to any business. It doesn't have to be set in stone, there's always room for flexibility as opportunities arise and you improve your business, but you do need to have one. To achieve millionaire mumpreneur status you have to be realistic about how you will get there. For example, if you set out to build a business around being a yoga teacher you either need to charge a huge amount to teach people the perfect sun salutation, or you need to create multiple income streams from virtual services, such as packaging your knowledge into products, e.g. DVDs, and building up your credibility.

Cash flow

As you have learned, the MMs in this book all continue to make big investments in themselves by attending events and hiring coaches. A big part of the work they will be doing when working with a coach is strategic planning, and they all have plans for new products, programmes and events that they will be doing throughout the coming year. This detailed planning also helps to manage and forecast cash flow. The beauty of a virtual business is that you can control cash flow much better, mostly by getting payment upfront and receiving recurring payments. For example, if you have created an information product, that anyone in the world can order through your website, customers pay for the order first and then you can either send it out yourself or use a fulfilment service. Alternatively, if it's a digital download the customer receives your product immediately after ordering. Another example is when selling group programmes or memberships. You can plan, set up and market them and have the orders taken online before the programme starts or you can receive monthly membership payments.

Watch your step

Alexis made an interesting point about only needing to see the next step. If you feel overwhelmed by the big leap to get to a million, and who wouldn't, envisage the bigger picture about what you want your life to look like to help you clarify your plan. Knowing where you want to be in, say, three or five years' time, what you will be doing and how you will be spending your time, will help you to see what you really want out of your business, and then you can track back to where you are now and start putting the building blocks into place. So, for you right now, maybe making a modest income from your business but having the

❝ Whatever you do, have a plan. ❞

flexibility to work from home and freedom to be there more for your kids is the most important plan. When you get to that place, and you start to slip into your comfort zone, that's when you can step it up and set yourself another milestone to reach.

Tax and legal implications

When you are planning your virtual business obviously you will need to find out about any tax and legal issues that might affect you. Even if you are going to start small with just an ezine and an eBook you still need to build a solid foundation to build on, so you will need to do some research about whether or not you want to have sole-trader status or set up as a limited company (which some customers may consider as more credible). Being a sole trader may seem like the easiest way to get started, but being a company has many advantages, including protecting your personal assets.

You should consider opening a separate bank account for your business transactions, understand what information you need to keep for tax purposes, get a qualified bookkeeper in as soon as possible, decide what insurance is appropriate, etc. You'll also need to think about protecting your business and that will require doing research, like whether you want to trademark your business name and how you can protect your intellectual property.

To sell services and products through your website your business will need to have easily accessible terms and conditions and you'll also need to have a merchant account with an online payment provider. You will be building a list of names and email addresses too, so you'll need to make your privacy policy clear to your website visitors. You should never sell or share their details with an unauthorised third party unless they opt-in to receive third-party information, and you have to make that very clear on your site. Get it right from the start and seek further support and advice from your local Business Link, your bank, business books, and online.

Time

Once you have all the basics in place you'll then need to plan your time. Take your business seriously and treat it like a business, not an expensive 'hobby' that you do in the evenings when the kids are in bed. When you are first setting up, working at night might be unavoidable, but that's not a sustainable situation for a successful business (or mum!).

Make the effort and continue to learn how to run a successful virtual business. It's crazy but some people who wouldn't dream of starting a real-world business, think they can easily make a go of an internet-based one. People will start an online venture on the premise that they no longer have to get up and go to work. They think they can simply work when they feel like it and still make a good living without having to work hard or put in long hours. Some people are seduced by the idea that running a successful virtual business is as easy as getting a website built, and expect to get customers simply by it existing. They couldn't be more wrong.

All of the MMs talked about taking a leap of faith. Some left well-paid careers and others really struggled to build their businesses, but they all made a commitment and weren't working on them in their spare time. So plan time for building your business. Some of that time has to be quiet with no distractions or interruptions. That's the only way you are going to be able to get a lot done in less time. Running a successful virtual business of any kind requires self-discipline. It didn't happen overnight for these MMs and it won't happen overnight for you, but you can certainly speed up the process by making a plan based on the proven success of others. Don't make the mistake of being totally unprepared for the investment of time that must be made in order for a virtual business to be successful. If you don't have a business background you need to, at the very minimum, get some good advice before you even consider starting. If you start off with a mindset of, 'I can work when I want to, I can get rich quick and I don't need a business plan', then that will guarantee failure.

Planning for chaos

The good news is you don't have to be a *really* organised person to make a success of running a business from home. You may not even find some of the business planning books and advice out there useful because they may not take into account the chaotic situation you are in. It's no use setting out to plan your business as if everything will run automatically smoothly and this is one of the reasons why I'm happy to use the word 'mumpreneur' to describe myself and these other mums, because the chaos of family life is intertwined with being an entrepreneur building a business.

Without a plan you'll go nowhere but this is more about organising the chaos rather than creating order. One way to make sure your plan works is to implement systems in both your family life and your business. From the point when everyone gets up in the morning have some kind of system for what happens, who does what and where things belong. In terms of your business that means having systems for marketing, sales, new customer enquiries, building customer relationships, dealing with complaints, following up leads, etc. You'll even need to have a system for simple tasks like writing your blog or posting an update on social media, e.g. spend just 15 minutes twice a day. Sometimes it can be the simplest system that makes a difference, such as checking your email at set times rather than constantly, which can be very distracting. Then you'll need to have a system for how you respond, e.g. immediately to each one, in order of priority, or replying to all new emails at a set time. So, plan for chaos!

SUCCESS MINDSET

I am an entrepreneur

Success doesn't happen by accident and it isn't just a lucky break. Success happens because of some very important factors. Success happened for these MMs using a virtual business model because they had the right strategies about internet marketing and the right mindset. Now, what's important to recognise is that they didn't start out thinking the way they do now.

Until the majority are entrepreneurs, then entrepreneurs will stand out as being different, thinking and acting differently from employees and the self-employed. I highlight the self-employed because there is a huge difference between thinking you are self-employed rather than an entrepreneur. With a self-employed mindset the emphasis is on 'self' and generally the self-employed person is doing a job they are experienced in or trained for and work for themselves. For example, a self-employed hairdresser may spend 80% of her time doing clients' hair and 20% of her time doing marketing and administration. Some days she is fully booked with customers but on others she may have only one or none. And what if she is sick or wants to take a holiday?

An entrepreneur builds a business that they can lead and expand, and put key people and systems in place to manage the day-to-day running of the business while they spend their time productively seeking new opportunities. If they are sick or take a holiday the business can still run like clockwork, customers are still served, money is still being made. So an entrepreneurial hairdresser would be figuring out all kinds of creative ways to provide a hairdressing service, hairdressing products and how to grow the business without being the only person doing the work. Think John Frieda. He was the first hairdresser in the UK to sell branded hair products on the high street and he built

> **" Success doesn't happen by accident and it isn't just a lucky break. "**

a hugely successful brand. Nowadays we have dozens of branded shampoos to choose from and many top hairdressers have achieved 'celebrity' status. An entrepreneur will have figured out a way to leverage their time, money and expertise to free themselves from the day-to-day tasks of managing their business. That's what a team is for!

I can do it

Another powerful mindset contributing to the success of these MMs is their acceptance of stepping into a bigger, bolder role of leadership. They were dissatisfied with comfortable and mediocre results. They acted on their dreams until eventually they had no choice but to become a reality. They got noticed by becoming impossible to ignore! Even when life was already good enough they still strived for better because they all believed so much in what they do. Their ambitions and accomplishments have nothing to do with greed and everything to do with authenticity. I want to share this beautiful piece from some writing by Marianne Williamson called 'A Return To Love':

Our deepest fear is not that we are inadequate

Our deepest fear is that we are powerful beyond measure

Your playing small does not serve the world

There is nothing enlightened about shrinking so that other people won't feel insecure around you

It says it all, but one of the most consistent limiting beliefs, and it's rampant in most people's lives to some degree, is 'I'm not good enough'. You may not even realise that this deep-seated belief is affecting your behaviour, but it could be stopping you from experiencing new relationships, opportunities, challenges and even happiness. You are on your own path; stop comparing yourself to and defining yourself by others, remind yourself how far you have come and look for evidence of what makes you already 'good enough'. It's already there.

Passion

In other words, what excites you? Maybe you don't need to define yourself by what you do as by who you are and what you are passionate about. Ideally there is a way for you to connect the three and create a business that really makes you want to jump out of bed in the morning! Okay, I'm over-egging it a bit but you get the point. This book is not about finding your 'dream job' because it doesn't exist, it's about creating a business that ideally combines your passion with your skills and gives you the freedom and flexibility you need for family life, and beyond. Start a business because you believe it will make money, but the goal is to make that money for a reason and to know what you are working for.

Think about all the things that you feel really passionate about. What stirs you up emotionally? Passion is an emotional state and it's being in that state while you are visualising starting and growing your business that will keep driving you. All the MMs have shown passion for their businesses. I would even suggest that without that passion there would be no business. But don't think that to be passionate you must be loud, expressive and high energy. While it's true that passion can manifest in that way, it can also be felt in a quiet and calm way, like the kind of passion you might feel when holding your newborn baby. What's important is that your passion can be channelled and drive you towards taking whatever action is necessary.

Instead of focusing on the problems you may be having around working or not working, focus on the solution. What can you do about it? What are you going to do about it? What options do you have? No problem has to be permanent if you are prepared to take the necessary action. To begin with, it could simply be the passion you have to be at home spending more time with your family and/or doing meaningful work that motivates you towards taking action. First you must believe it's possible. You *choose* what you believe and there is always a way to turn things around if you are committed and if you have passion.

SUCCESSFUL COLLABORATION

Building a successful virtual business has many things in common with the building of a successful brick and mortar one, although there are significant differences as well. The saying, 'It's not what you know, it's who you know that counts' is true for any business. Building good, solid relationships is an important aspect of building a successful internet enterprise.

Relationships

It's important to put yourself into situations where you will meet others who have businesses that are similar or complimentary to yours so that you can develop relationships and collaborate with others. Attending seminars or conferences is a great way to build friendly business relationships.

The MMs in this book have all cultivated relationships within their field, which has helped them to grow their businesses by doing joint ventures and recruiting affiliates. They have been able to leverage the expertise of others to bring more value to their customers and community and in turn have been able to share their expertise.

Social networking

Social networking is an amazing tool for collaboration. Through sites like Facebook and Twitter it's possible to build a network, share ideas and information, get to know, like and trust someone and ultimately figure out a way to work with someone you admire and respect. As you would expect, all of these MMs have a really strong online brand and presence in social media. Showing people who they are and what they are all about encourages collaboration in just a few clicks! It also takes away the 'CEO in the ivory tower' perception because you get to see some of the real people behind the business.

Cooperation

This attitude of cooperation is a refreshing change from the classic competitive one. The economy is changing and we are moving towards a cooperative world because the source of all opportunity comes from other people. Everything you need in business and in life comes from other people and if you believe that you are always competing in business you will be expressing negative emotions like envy, which is unattractive. There will be competition out there, there will be others serving the same target market or offering a similar service to yours, but it's how you perceive them and what you decide it means to your business that makes the difference. There is always room for another, if you find a way to be different.

See your competition as someone you could potentially collaborate with. There may be many ways you could actually support each other that help you both grow. If you do feel some envy when a competitor is seen to be achieving some great success take it as a sign that you would like to accomplish more and use it as an opportunity to step up your business.

Fabienne is in an extremely crowded market. How many businesses and resources are there offering marketing advice and training? Exactly! Fabienne has done it her way and continues to expand her client-attraction business even with a world of competition.

Rewarding the cooperation of others is a successful strategy that many internet marketers, including the MMs, use in their businesses through an affiliate programme, where commissions are paid to people who refer sales. People are usually happy to spread the word about a product or service they found useful and an affiliate programme simply takes the word of mouth one step further and rewards cooperation.

SUCCESSFULLY INVESTING – IN YOURSELF

Growth and expansion are necessary for any business to survive and sometimes these terms are a bit misunderstood. Their most obvious meaning is to get bigger and broader but that is not the only definition that applies. Growth, for example, can mean gaining knowledge and becoming wiser, and expansion can mean broadening the knowledge base from which a company operates. Nothing ever stays the same. Change is the only certainty in the world. What was hot or what worked yesterday is old news today and it will be ancient history tomorrow. Entrepreneurs must grow with and adapt to changes as they happen and on the internet change happens quickly.

So what is the key to growth and expansion of a virtual business?

When a traditional brick business grows and expands, it builds or leases a bigger building and hires more employees, but that doesn't apply to an internet-based business. The key to growth and expansion of an online business is for the business owner to always and continuously invest in them. They must be willing to stay on the cutting edge of technology and they must be willing to accept and adapt to changes as they occur. Internet businesses are not buildings. Internet businesses like these are people. They only grow when the person who is driving that business invests in her own knowledge, personal development and ability. Invest in yourself. Your business is you, your computer, your team and a broadband connection, so you could actually operate your virtual business from anywhere.

Your business is based upon your own knowledge and your ability. Those are the company 'assets' and those are the ones that need to grow and expand constantly so that your business thrives. Expansion and growth are imperative to survival and for an internet business that means expanding and growing the knowledge of the person running the company...you! You must stay on top of new technology and you must expand your knowledge base about your own area of expertise.

Things change fast. New information becomes available every day. Consistently putting in the effort to stay on top of things will almost certainly prevent you from falling behind. Keeping up is easier than catching up and if you keep up, you can usually find a way to forge ahead.

Keeping up

So how's a mum working from home supposed to keep up? Well, the good news is that there are plenty of online resources on offer. You could participate in tele-seminars or webinars that are related to your business. You will learn a lot, of course, but equally important, you will come into contact with those who are already succeeding in the niche market that you are working in. My experience of working from home is that at times you can feel very isolated so it's important to get out there in the real world sometimes. Attending seminars, conferences and events gives you access to experts who are in a position to help you and will give you all the information you need to succeed, plus you get to network with new friends and contacts.

A valuable asset that any new entrepreneur needs is a good and capable mentor. Someone who has already made all of the mistakes and can help you to avoid making them yourself. A mentor can come in many forms and to begin with reading books, like this one, may give you access to one. As time goes by your mentors could be contacts you meet along the way or coaches you hire. All the MMs have their own coaching programmes and their clients pay a premium to be coached personally by them.

> " Keeping up is easier than catching up. "

Why would anyone who has already built a successful internet business want to spend their time helping a newbie succeed?

The people who are the most successful are the ones, amazingly enough, who are the most likely to mentor an up-and-coming entrepreneur, but successful marketers are not going to be interested in wasting their time on a person who has not already worked hard to lay the foundation themselves and shown commitment. Mentors want to see that you have the right mindset, are working hard at leveraging yourself, are helping yourself and that you are well aware of how important taking action is.

You might just need someone to help nudge you out of your comfort zone. We all have one and it's very tempting to keep on doing the things that we have always done in the same way we have always done them. You must be willing to leave your own comfort zone. Just because what has worked before is still currently working doesn't mean that there aren't newer, better and more efficient ways of doing them. That's one of the great advantages of working with a coach who can help you to see how you could be more effective. Take advantage of all the information that's out there, learn it and apply it to your virtual business.

RISKING SUCCESS

New is not always better and the only way to tell is by investigating new ideas yourself and then adapting the ones that can help you to grow your business. Investing in yourself will increase your knowledge and confidence, so don't be afraid of trying new things and new ways of doing things. This is one of the secrets to success.

...and failure

The success (or failure) of your business really is up to you now. If you succeed, the credit will all belong to you, and if you fail, you will own that as well. Fear of failure is so hard-wired into us that it can stop even the most competent and qualified amongst us from taking the leap. What's the worst-case scenario? Supposing you were to jump in at the deep end, hand in your notice and start a business with no income for, say, six months. Could you survive that? What might you learn in those six months about the reality, not fantasy of business? Would that temporary period have a permanent impact on your finances? How quickly could you recover and re-coup your start-up costs to get back on track?

Success and failure are two sides of the same coin. You don't want to flip that coin into the air and leave it to chance as to which side it lands. You want complete control over the fate of your business and you do have that control. Every decision will be yours to make. If you make wise choices then you can celebrate success. If you make unwise choices then your virtual business could be put into jeopardy and you'll then have to decide how you are going to react to that and how you are going to turn things around.

Start small but think big

Every day thousands of internet businesses are launched all over the world and so too are many traditional ones. How many of those companies will be around in one year's time, never mind five years? You can increase your chances of success by simply following the guidelines that are available in this book and the many resources and mentors there are out there to help you. Don't try and figure it all out by yourself. Find out what works and do it.

To save yourself some sleepless nights when starting out, start small but think big. The technology you need is not prohibitive and for the cost of an average family holiday you could be up and running very quickly. There will be small risks to consider on a daily basis that will affect your cash flow, such as whether you should spend money on a marketing campaign to generate more business but risk not getting any results. Reduce the risks involved by educating yourself as much as possible but remember that you'll never completely eliminate risk. Even walking across the road is a risk!

66 Start small but think big. 99

SUCCESSFUL VIRTUAL TEAM

When you work in a job that pays you for the hours of work that you do, you get into a work=money mindset. After all, when you work for others, work does equal money. But when you launch a virtual business the rules can change, if you want them to, and the 'work' that used to make you money now prevents you from making money. The work you are doing that you once got paid to do, like answering the telephone, replying to emails, seeing clients, etc, is actually preventing you from making the deals that will make the money in your business.

Work does not equal money

Thinking of employment as the way to make money is actually counterproductive to building a successful virtual business. But it's easy to understand why we get into this mindset. We have been living with the concept since we were kids. Think about it. What was your first job? Did you do chores in return for some pocket money? Did you get money after you had done the work? You weren't being paid to think and plan, to find a more effective way of doing the chore, or to look for a new market for what you were doing. You were being paid to do the set task. Again, work did in fact equal money.

To build a successful virtual business you need to not be doing the 'work'. The work isn't what will make the money for you. The work must still be done but you don't have to be the one doing it. Build your team, virtual or not, then you need to be looking for the deals that will make you money. So what is 'work' in a virtual business? The usual day-to-day tasks that make any business function; telephone calls must be answered, emails must be read and responded to, paperwork must be dealt with, files must be kept orderly, the list goes on and on, but this is just 'work'.

Nobody is going to pay you to answer the phone, read emails or file paperwork. It isn't making you any money and it most certainly is not where you should be focusing your energy. Once your virtual business is up and running, it's a very wise investment to pay a virtual assistant to do this for you. This sets you free to make the deals that actually make you money and help your business to thrive. Realistically you can't do that right away, but have that awareness from the start.

In addition, customer service is vital work in any business. It must be done quickly, efficiently and above all competently. It might well be work that in the beginning, at least, you must do it yourself. However, there are plenty of online services that are perfectly capable of handling this work for you. Don't make it harder on yourself!

Tasks that could be outsourced

- Answering calls and dealing with enquiries.

- Answering email enquiries and sending emails on your behalf.

- Making reservations, booking appointments in your diary and planning events.

- Assisting with email marketing, campaigns and customer-relationship management.

- Bookkeeping, analysing results and keeping track of cash flow.

- Technical support, search-engine optimisation and website-statistics analysis.

All the daily tasks will probably have to be done by you until you can either take the decision – or afford – to outsource some support. To start with you are likely to wear all of the hats in your business, but at least you can learn how to work smarter and train others. You can learn how to get the same amount accomplished in less time, e.g. use automation and make your website work for you as much as possible from the start.

Work smart

Working smart will give you the flexibility that you are looking for. Your kids will have different needs as they get older and you'll always have the challenge of working out how everyone's demands can be met. It might mean having to put your head down to meet a deadline to allow you to take time out during the school holidays. It ebbs and flows. Trying to run your family and your business under one roof is definitely a challenge and doing it all yourself isn't sustainable. Trying to run a business in the evenings might seem like your only option at first, but remind yourself why you wanted to start a business from home. The chances are that flexibility is one of the reasons and yes, you will have the flexibility to work in the evenings and at weekends, but that's not going to give you any more time and may not be the time when you can give the best energy to your work. Ultimately, if you want the flexibility to work the hours that fit your life you will need to start building up a team to help you achieve that.

Remember: you don't have to do it all yourself, you choose to do it all yourself. Be aware of the consequences of that choice. You will be very good at some things and not so good at others. That's okay. Accept it, do more of what you're good at and then delegate the rest.

Share the load

Fabienne is very open about what it means to her to outsource all kinds of support both domestic and business. She thinks the reason why so many mums fall into the trap of doing it all is because they "want to be a good wife and mother" and that doing everything is a way of demonstrating that. That belief can easily backfire when you soon feel exhausted. As Fabienne explains:

> When I'm resentful, overwhelmed, and feel like I'm running two jobs, I get resentful and think, 'When is it ever going to be about me?' I feel like slamming a door. That doesn't make for a happy husband, happy kids or a happy home and it doesn't show a good example, so I learned how to ask for help. I realised that it doesn't mean I'm weak. It's not a reflection on me as a mother or a career woman if I need to ask for help. There are people out there who want to help you.

Let's not forget that support for you and your business can come from your own family. Being around the home more while you are running your own business is the ideal opportunity for you to teach your children how to do some household chores. You are at home but your day isn't about doing the housework now that you have a business to run. However, the laundry isn't going to do itself. Getting your kids to make their own bed, do their own laundry and make their own lunch boxes can be done from a young age and could make a big difference. It all comes down to teaching them life skills and empowering them so they can be self-sufficient.

And what about your husband or partner? What skills can they bring to the party? Do they want to be involved? Maybe this could be the start of an entrepreneurial family life that brings together everyone's strengths, with the same goal: to make a success of your business and create wealth. After all, everyone in the family will benefit when you have made a million!

Be a role model

Think about the difference in a mum coming home from a job that is burning her out, that she finds frustrating, and she resents. She's always complaining and taking it out on everyone in the family. What message is that giving to her kids? What meaning could the children be giving to mum working? Mum working means she is always tired, snappy and doesn't have time for me.

What is this woman modelling for her kids compared to a mum who may be busy and happy running a business from home but sometimes feels a little guilty for checking email while the kids are around? What are we showing our children, our daughters, about what it means to work and raise a family?

Maybe in choosing to run our own businesses from home we're showing them that you can do what you love, make a great living, contribute, be happy and be there more for your kids, and that it is possible. Maybe we'll have to wait and see because things were different when we were children. Our mothers never had an opportunity like this and the MMs and all the other mumpreneurs around the world could be setting a new standard. Breaking the mould. Our kids are learning so much just by watching what we're doing and being around it. Can having an entrepreneurial mum who is running an online business from home be beneficial for a child? I'll have to get back to you on that one in about ten years. Maybe that's a whole new book!

What do you need?

Building a virtual team and using automation to support your business is going to give you the freedom you want. It's about being able to be there for your kids. It's about being able to have the relationship you want with your spouse or partner. It's even about having the time to get out and exercise – remember what that is? Go running in the middle of the day if that's what you need. It's about taking care of you.

Give yourself permission because taking care of you doesn't mean you are neglecting your children. Paradoxically, taking care of you probably means your children are also better taken care of. So get the support you need and don't feel guilty about asking for help or taking up offers of help.

> 66 Taking care of you doesn't mean you are neglecting your children. 99

WHAT DO YOU WANT, DO YOU REALLY, REALLY WANT?

Until now we have focused on what a virtual business is all about and success stories of mums from all over the world who are making this business model work. You have some idea of the practicalities of building a virtual business but you are also aware of how important your thoughts are because ultimately they will determine the actions that you are willing to take. The clues to what you really want lie in subtle feelings that you need to be tuned in to. The problem with living on a crazy treadmill everyday, with no time and space, running on adrenaline and flopping down with exhaustion at the end of each day is that very often we are simply too overwhelmed to feel the inspiration, passion and motivation needed to drive us to take action. My maternity leave gave me the time and space I needed to evaluate my priorities and the life I really wanted. You must know what you want so you can start working for it and there's a big difference between what you want and what you think you can have. It comes back to the 'I'm not good enough' limiting belief. Go for what you actually want.

What? You feel guilty for wanting your life to be better somehow? You think you should automatically be happy with your lot? What is it with mums and guilt? I want to share something with you that made a big impact on me and helped me enormously with the guilt issue. There is 'good' guilt and 'bad' guilt. How you interpret the guilt you feel can change your feelings in an instant. To decide whether the guilt you feel is good or bad ask yourself if you will regret your decision or whether you think you should be doing something based on other people's expectations. When you are being true to your self, good guilt can be positive. For example, you might feel guilty about working 60 hours a week in a job you now resent because you would like to spend more time with your family. Good guilt or bad guilt? Or you feel guilty about giving up a stimulating and rewarding career that contributed massively to the household income to now stay at home full-time with your children. Good guilt or bad guilt? Perhaps you feel guilty about using some savings or getting a bank loan to take the risk of starting your own business against the advice of others. Good guilt or bad guilt? What about feeling guilty about returning to work soon after having your baby to a job or business you absolutely love? Good guilt or bad guilt? Simply ask yourself: "Will I regret doing this? Will I regret spending time or money on this?"

Becoming a mother can cause a massive shift in perspective and really make you question your life's purpose. Whether you are spending your entire week at work or at home with your children you may feel like something's missing: your purpose. For many, a career and a family are not enough any more. We want to make a difference. We want a purpose to our life that is bigger than us and it's not just about money. It's about what we can do with money. It's about the freedom to choose meaningful and deeply fulfilling work. We just need some help realising that we can have what we want and keep our priority to our families intact.

Before you read this book what was your perception of a business woman with children making a million? A high-flier in the City working 60 hours a week and never being home for bedtime stories? Power suit and stilettos, breakfast meetings, boardrooms, boarding schools and au pairs? This book smashes that stereotype and proves that it's possible to create a business from home, from scratch, from passion and be around to do the school run, play dates and even have time for yourself. A great thing about building a virtual business is there's no need for hair drying, heels and handbags. Every day is 'casual Friday' if you want it to be! Okay, that sounds flippant but the point is you have the freedom to be who you want to be. Living your purpose is energising, not draining. So if you thought making a million from a home-based business was impossible then remember Roger Bannister. The four-minute mile was considered impossible before he achieved it, and now many athletes have done it! So, too, there's a new standard for mumpreners; making a million is possible. It has been done over and over again. It's being proven by women just like you.

Women who made a decision and followed through, who are making a difference and living their purpose.

So, what is it that you really want?

What do you mean you don't know? Panic not, that's a good start! The thing is sometimes it's okay not to know. What I mean is you don't need to know right now exactly what will happen for you to get what you really want. Opportunities will come to you from people you haven't met yet, deals you haven't done yet, places you haven't been yet. You don't need to know the specific details, you just need to know that you can trust yourself to get there. In other words, you need to take a leap of faith to get anywhere close to what you really want. All the MMs talk about taking a leap of faith, having faith and honouring their faith at some point in their journey, so I guess we must take notice of how important it is to success. I think we are all aware that anything really worth doing or having requires a leap of faith. Faith is simply a state of mind. Starting a business with an uncertain outcome requires taking a leap of faith so what's stopping us from taking that leap? Fear. The security of a mediocre present is more comfortable than the journey to a successful, extraordinary, outstanding future. Taking a leap of faith requires not knowing what will happen. It might help you to think about whether you feel pushed into making a decision or pulled towards making a decision. Allowing yourself to be pulled towards what you really want will energise you and that energy will keep you going as you turn your desires into positive action.

When you are going through the process sometimes it's easier to think about what you want in terms of material possessions, e.g. a bigger house, or circumstances, e.g. working part-time from home, but you may give no thought to or have no idea about who you really want to be. Getting more stuff or settling for boring and unchallenging work just because you can do it from home will not fulfil you. You must be clear about what is most important to you and then set out to live by

> **" Starting a business with an uncertain outcome requires taking a leap of faith so what's stopping us from taking that leap? Fear. "**

those values. They guide you to make certain decisions and actions which shape your life and it's only by living by your values that you will get to a place of complete fulfilment.

Anything that is important to you in life is a value, and when you have difficulty in making big decisions it's usually because you are unclear about what you value most or you have a conflict in your values. For example, your family and security may be high values for you, but freedom and adventure may be too. Can you see how not finding a way to live by all these values might make you feel either restless, frustrated or resentful?

The really big life values can be described as either ends or means values. What we truly want in our lives comes down to a personal mix of emotional states – the ends – and there are various ways for us to achieve these emotional states – the means. So your family is one of the most important values to you but to get to the end value ask yourself, 'What does having my family give me?' The answer could be love, security, happiness, peace, passion, comfort, etc. Your core values are made up of the different emotional states that you want to experience consistently in life. To be truly happy we must know the difference between pursuing our means values without paying attention to our more important end values. For example, imagine two of your highest values were inspiration and contribution and you chose to become a teacher as a means of living by those values. At first you feel like you are truly making a difference to the lives of the children and you feel good, but as your career develops you spend more time on administration, in meetings, and on procedures, to the point where you no longer teach. You set out with the intention of being a teacher, achieved your goal and originally had the means to live by your end values of inspiration and contribution, but now you have ended up thinking, 'There's got to be more to life than this!' You need to find a way to get back to living by your true values. It doesn't necessarily mean quitting your job or doing anything too drastic; sometimes just a few simple changes to the way you work or exploring other ways to live by those values could be the solution.

How to discover what's important to you

My values

Think about the most important things in your life. It's okay at first to think about the means, e.g. my family, but then ask yourself, 'What does having my family do for me/give me?' to get to the end value. Don't question anything. There are no right or wrong answers. This exercise is here to help you make decisions to lead you into your ideal life. Repeat this process until you have a list of ten end values.

1.

2.

3.

4.

5.

6.

7.

8.

9.

10.

Now you have your ten core values and we'll come back to your list to make it even more powerful for you.

Okay, let's go back to conflicting values because this is usually at the core of the 'how to combine family life with working' dilemma for so many mums. If some of our end values include love, security, freedom, success and comfort, then if we are living our lives to satisfy only some criteria, there is the potential to feel emotional pain by not finding a way to satisfy the others. Maybe you chose to quit your career to stay at home with your children because you value comfort and security but you also value success, freedom and power. How do you think you might feel if you had no way to satisfy those other big life values? Maybe you now value security more than success and that's how you feel comfortable about making your decision, which is usually what people do, mostly without realising it!

We put our values into a hierarchy because it's fair to say that even though we have different core values we often don't value them all equally. There are some end values that we will do more to achieve than others; it's certainly possible that you may value love and security over success and freedom. Take a moment to revist your core values list and re-write them into a hierarchy, with number one being the most important to you right now. If you are struggling to choose the importance of one over the other, ask yourself which one you would choose if you had to.

My values hierarchy

1.

2.

3.

4.

5.

6.

7.

8.

9.

10.

Take a moment to look over your values. What have you learned about the important aspects in your life? Can you see how needing to live by your highest end value, to feel that emotional state consistently, shapes the decisions you make and the direction your life takes? Can you see how someone whose number-one value is security may make completely different life decisions compared to someone whose top value is freedom? Knowing your values hierarchy is so important because your top values are those that will bring you the most happiness and fulfilment, and your values may be very different from other mums within your community, family and friends. Now, the ultimate experience is to be living our lives by meeting all of our top core values simultaneously. There is always a way to satisfy all our values. We just need to find it!

The first time I was introduced to the concept of values was when I first discovered Neuro-Linguistic Programming (NLP) in 2000, and as I progressed to become a Master Practitioner, working with values was a constant. In my sales training career I touched on identifying values during various courses but it was Tony Robbins, www.anthonyrobbins.com, who really focused my mind on understanding values and using that knowledge to really shape your life. I had enjoyed studying his work and reading his books but it was going to one of his life-changing weekend seminars that has had a lasting impact. That weekend I not only walked on fire but I learned the most powerful information that I have ever learned about values.

Changing your values to change your life

What would happen if instead of simply knowing what your values were you purposefully selected and switched the order of them based on the life you really want to live? You see, for most of us our current values are the result of a life of conditioning, usually from external sources. All our lives we have received messages from our family, friends, partners, community, government and even the media, that have unconsciously been programmed into us. We have formed beliefs about ourselves and the world from this conditioning and our values are also formed from it. Have you ever stopped to question why you think a certain way about something? Is that truly what you believe or have you just inherited or absorbed that belief from another person?

It's possible that some of our most important values could be a result of what we think we should feel or how we think we should live our lives. Tony says, "We are not our values. We are much more than or values", and even though you may think your values are great the chances are you didn't create them through purposeful choices or from a master plan of how you want your ideal life to be. If you've chosen to stay at home to raise your family but feel unfulfilled and restless yet your top values include love and security, it's possible that you feel that you should stay at home and that the only way to feel and give love and security is to be a stay at home mum – based on other people's expectations.

What if you could create a new set of values that you have purposefully chosen to guide you towards living your ultimate, ideal life?

In order to live your best, most fulfilling, most extraordinary life and really make a difference, switching your values could be the key. Tony's exercise in changing your values to change your life involves either adding values to help you accomplish your ideal life or eliminating those which may be holding you back. You have chosen this book because on some level you are attracted to the idea of being a millionaire mumpreneur and you are curious enough to investigate further. I hope you have found the stories inspiring and that you feel compelled to take action, but your list of values could actually be holding you back from creating the life you really want. Here's how: Let's say you are a stay at home mum and because one of your highest values is security you made the decision to stay at home and raise your children. So far so good, but then you find yourself feeling like you are lacking in achievements, you are not satisfying your life's purpose, you would like to contribute more, you know you can contribute so much more yet you just don't know how you will ever be successful. Now, the security you wanted by staying at home with your children feels stifling. You still value security so how can you feel secure and give security? What can you do differently? Take a look at your values list and add success. In fact put it right at the top. Your number one value: Success.

How does making success your most important value make you feel? Excited? Scared? Motivated? Free? Only you know, but the point is that now you have shifted your values you can now purposefully start attracting success into your life. Maybe the financial rewards that success could bring mean you can give financial security in addition to emotional security to your children. Maybe the success will make you feel more secure in yourself. You see, there is always a way to live your life satisfying your values simultaneously. You just have to find it.

Can you see how some of these MMs have created an ideal life according to their values? They own businesses that give purpose and meaning to their lives, they have schedules that allow them to be there more for their children, they have the freedom to make decisions and to express their passion, they have the adventure of new opportunities and they have the flexibility to make time for intimacy with their partner and to take care of their health. If what you really, really want sounds something like this, then what values might you have to add or eliminate? Take a look at your values again and make a new list of purposeful values.

My new values

1.

2.

3.

4.

5.

6.

7.

8.

9.

10.

Now your list is complete, notice how you feel but beware of allowing feelings of fear, worry and 'I'm not good enough' to destroy your new purposeful life plan. Yes, problems will always be there but only focusing on solutions, not worrying, will help you to get where you really want to be – faster.

What do you really, really want power questions

Use these power questions to help you discover your true purpose, ideal life and what you really want:

- What do I really, really want?

- What's the ideal situation?

- What is most important to me?

- What's important about that?

- What will having that do for me?

- What would it look like?

- What do I have to give?

- What would make a huge difference?

- What is the right thing to do?

- What is the next step?

- What am I avoiding?

- What's stopping me?

- What's the worst that could happen if I did this?

- What are the consequences of me not doing this?

- What am I denying myself?

- What do I need to do differently?

- What am I not facing up to?

- What other options do I have?

- How does this apply to my life?

- Who do I want to be?

- What would I do if I were certain not to fail?

- What does success look like to me?

- What is my vision for my family?

- What difference would this make?

- Who can guide me?

Take action!

The reasons that a new internet entrepreneur might 'fail' could be narrowed down to four possibilities:

1. They didn't have the right mindset.

2. They didn't have a solid foundation.

3. They didn't know how to grow and expand the business.

4. They didn't plan for success.

You need information and the best way to get it is to simply ask questions of those who have the answers.

There are plenty of courses, programmes and coaching available, both on and offline, purposefully designed to help you understand how to set up and run a successful internet business, so there are no excuses there! Investing in a coaching programme or mastermind group could help you avoid mistakes, keep you on track and encourage you to grow.

Remember, YOU are your business.

Continuing to keep yourself educated and informed is not a choice if your business is to be successful. You know that all the MMs are constantly learning new things and applying those new ideas and strategies in their businesses. They attend real world seminars. They attend tele-seminars and webinars. They read. They learn. They grow. They adapt. And, crucially, they succeed. To live is to learn.

We live in unprecedented times. A time when technology has given us freedom to break the rules about combining work and family. A time when we are free to create our ideal life based on our passions and purpose, and not based on either our own or other people's expectations of us. Thousands of people every week are starting up businesses, some of them far less capable than you. You can either decide not to do something out of fear or you can decide to do the same thing out of courage. Demonstrate to your children what's possible in life by being an example of living your life on your terms. You are stronger and more capable than you ever thought possible.

CONCLUSION

There's no such thing as the perfect business, the perfect job, or the perfect life. Perfect is too rigid, as if once you have reached perfection (and you never will by the way, sorry!), there is no further improvement required. Instead, aim for ideal. A virtual business is an ideal way for mums to combine doing what they love with raising their family. It's an ideal way for mums to have financial independence, be resourceful and self-reliant. The ultimate challenge is to take action and really make it work. You might be tempted to think, 'Why even bother? What difference will it make anyway?' You feel helpless and nothing will stop you more from taking action than a feeling of helplessness. Having got this far in the book you will know that only by taking action, against all odds and in spite of fear, will you ever be able to make a difference.

So action is the key and I'd like to share with you something I have learned about three keys to success:

1. **Contribution.** Everyone has something to contribute.

2. **Communication strategy.** What are all the different ways that you can get your message out there?

3. **Commitment to action.** You can have expertise to contribute and a great communication strategy, but if you don't have a commitment to act and follow through, you won't succeed.

Fabienne would encourage, no, demand, that you take a no-excuses approach, just as she did:

> *I am going to take a no-excuses approach to making six figures or hitting and exceeding the million-dollar mark. If I made a commitment to doing that without sacrificing my family, my happiness or any other part of my life, I would feel like I'd hit the jackpot.*

She admits she used to feel resentment about having a family and thought that was holding her back from achieving success:

Very few people talk about that resentment of, 'If I were single or we didn't have kids, I would be so much further along'. It doesn't have to be that way and it is a really limiting way to live. Say to yourself, 'I'm going to do this to the best of my ability, support, focus and dedication'. You can make a lot of money and be happy in all aspects of your life as well. Not taking action is usually because you're afraid of making a mistake or think you are lacking in ability. Say to yourself 'Whatever happens I'm going to learn from it because it's going to move me forward'.

I've made plenty of mistakes while building my business, still do, but it's always the things that haven't worked out the way I wanted that I learned the most from, and they've actually helped to move me forward much more quickly.

Fear

It's important to recognise whether you have a real fear or a perceived fear because there is a huge difference. The fear of falling off a tall building is a real fear. We are certain that something terrible will happen if we do; we may even die. That kind of real fear is hard-wired into us all as a protection mechanism. A perceived fear is different. We are uncertain and that's scary. We might be afraid to launch a new business in case it fails. You agonise over your decision thinking, 'I've never done this before. I'm afraid to do it because I don't know what will happen'. That kind of perceived fear is also there to protect us, to keep us safe, but it can also end up ruining our chances of really experiencing life.

You were probably terrified of having your first baby. You didn't know what was going to happen. You'd never done it before but you were probably reassured by the knowledge that so many women have. Maybe you read one of the numerous parenting books so you had an idea of what to expect. You probably found it invaluable to talk to fellow parents about their experiences and have found yourself applying some of the same parenting strategies that you have seen work well in other families. In other words, you have been modelling. Now you know that the same modelling and learning process that you have been through by becoming a mother for the first time can be applied to starting your own business for the first time too.

Follow the leader

You have also leaned the importance of peer groups, so there's no time like the present to reach out to other mums who also want to be successful, start a business and be at home to see more of their kids. There are communities out there of mums just like you; I know I've created one, take a look at www.supermummy.com and join my mumpreneur social network to get you started. Why not give yourself a head start and invest in a mentor or a coach now? Find someone who has already travelled that path and can show you the way, show you what's possible because it can be really frustrating when there is no one to guide you and you feel like you just can't do it.

Reading this book has been a great start because when you are aware of someone just like you doing it and showing you how you can do it too, suddenly your world opens up to a new opportunity and you see the possibilities.

It doesn't have to be so difficult if you follow others before you because the path is already there. You simply follow in their tracks. There are plenty of coaches out there doing an amazing job of showing women that it's right there in front of them, and some of them are right here in this book. You just have to be shown the way. When you achieve business success you unconsciously inspire other mums to do it too. It creates the possibility for others to step up and be willing to do it for themselves. By making your life better you have also helped make it possible for other mums to make their life better too.

What do I want?

What would make your life better? Think in terms of what excites you rather than the goals you want to reach. If you could do anything you wanted and had a guarantee that you wouldn't fail what would you do? Is accepting boredom and frustration and giving up hope on ever doing what you really want to do better than at least trying? Don't you owe it to yourself and to your kids to live your ideal life? To be proud of who you really are? That's the real meaning of success isn't it? It's not about what we have got, or what we have done, it's really about who we are. It's knowing that you're living your life in a way that's authentic to who you really are meant to be and who you want to be. That's success. Making a million isn't enough to make you feel happy, fulfilled and secure. Who you are will have more effect on your life than what you've got. Take some time to understand who you are, what you need and what you really want, then liberate yourself to go after it.

Still risky

Don't want to risk it? Maybe we should look at risk again because you have learned that all the MMs have taken risks and now even purposefully put themselves into uncomfortable positions knowing that those risks will help them to stretch, expand and grow. They have conditioned themselves to overcome discomfort and move on. We decide if something is risky or not depending on our references, either personal or other peoples'. So if you have already experienced something that could be considered risky and the outcome was okay then you have a positive reference for that situation if it ever came up again. For example, having a baby can be risky but you would have known that the majority of births result in a healthy baby, a positive outcome. You are taking a risk by having a baby but are reassured by other people's references and use that to help you. Then after experiencing birth yourself and linking the risk you took to the reward of a beautiful baby, you now have your own positive reference that helps you go on to have more babies!

The way you use references will determine whether you see something as a risk. For some mums, starting a business from home doing something they love might not be as big a risk as re-training for a new career or going through a series of job interviews. The worst that could happen might not be failing miserably, it could be having to accept that you never even tried.

Be yourself

Not everybody will have resonated with every mumpreneur story in this book, but I hope you identified with even just a couple of these women, learned from them and were inspired by their stories. Modelling the success of others can save you years of struggle, frustration and be a short-cut to re-invention. Ultimately that's what this new experience of building a business from home is going to be all about. You re-inventing yourself. Give yourself permission to step aside from previous labels that you have put on yourself, or allowed others to put on you, and decide who you really want to be. Commit to your new mumpreneur identity, or whatever identity feels right for you, and communicate that to everyone. Use your new identity at every opportunity and get comfortable with it so that it really feels a part of you. You have already been through this when you took on the new identity of 'mum' but this is your opportunity to give yourself the identity of who you are now and who you want to become, not who you were. Leave the past behind you and embrace your new identity.

APPENDIX

7 GREAT REASONS TO START AN EZINE

1   It's a way of capturing the email addresses of your website visitors which gives you permission to contact them again.

2.   Saves money (no printing) and time (no postage).

3.   Demonstrates to your current clients and prospects everything you have to offer them.

4.   Builds a loyal base of followers who are ready to work with you, buy from you and promote you to others.

5.   Keeps you in touch with all of your customers and prospects on a regular basis.

6.   Attracts potential partners, endorsement requests, interviews, speaking invitations and other opportunities.

7.   Packages what you know into tips and articles for your customers and prospects. When they are ready and need or want your products or services they'll come straight to you.

Ezines can be created from a template or by having a custom template designed, and can be created in and sent from autoresponder software such as:

*   www.aweber.com

*   www.constantcontact.com

*   www.1shoppingcart.com

7 STEPS TO CREATING AN EBOOK

1   In a text editor create a cover page including title, author name, logo, photos or graphics and a brief description

2. Add an 'About the author' page, which tells your story and promotes the benefits of your product or service

3. Create a table of contents

4. Create your chapters or step-by-step instructions

5. Include an upsell at the end for other products and services

6. Add a disclaimer to avoid any legal issues from your advice

7. Convert to a pdf

Cover graphics to promote your eBook or any other information products can be outsourced to a graphic designer such as:

*   www.killercovers.com

RECOMMENDED RESOURCES

Please note: I recommend these resources but do not accept responsibility for any purchase you make through them.

Creating online audio

- www.audioacrobat.com

All-in-one shopping cart, auto-responders, credit card processing, and internet marketing tools

- www.1shoppingcart.com

Tele-seminar providers

- www.instantteleseminar.com
- www.conferencegenie.com

Webinar providers

- www.dimdm.com
- www.citrixonline.com
- www.gotowebinar.com

Video conferencing providers

- www.skype.com
- www.oovoo.com

Video sharing

- www.youtube.com
- www.viddler.com

Membership software

- www.membergate.com

Online scheduling software

- www.appointment-plus.com
- http://timedriver.timetrade.com

Online Surveys

- www.surveymonkey.com

Online invoicing and expenses service

- www.freshbooks.com

Outsourcing - technical

- www.scriptlance.com
- www.guru.com
- www.odesk.com

Outsourcing – administration

- www.assistu.com
- www.virtuallysorted.com

Outsourcing – telephone calls

- www.virtual-receptionist.com

FURTHER READING

The 4-Hour Work Week by Timothy Ferris

The e Myth Revisited: Why Most Small Businesses Don't Work and What To Do About It by Michael E Gerber

POP: Stand Out In Any Crowd by Sam Horn

Supermummy: The Ultimate Mumpreneur's Guide To Online Business Success by Mel McGee

Start Your Own Information Marketing Business by Entrepreneur Press and Robert Skrob

Think and Grow Rich by Napoleon Hill

Tribes by Seth Godin